INFLUENCER
INCORPORATED

living a life of influence
in a world of control

A. G. "Pete" Hinojosa

published by

CREATIVE
communication PUBLICATIONS

atlanta, georgia

Influencer Incorporated

Published by CreativeCommunication Publications
        Atlanta, Georgia USA
Distributed by Omega Quest • *www.apurposefuljourney.com*
        Houston, Texas USA
Layout and design: Chris Carey • *www.ChrisCarey.com*
Edited by M. Kay duPont, CSP, CPDT • *www.tcc-wsa.com*
Cover Illustration by Digital Vision and Chris Carey

DISCLAIMER: The purpose of this book is to provide insight regarding self-improvement and personal improvement. It is not meant to replace professional counseling. Referral to a qualified counselor is recommended for issues outside the scope of this publication, which is intended only for general use and not as a specific course of treatment.

ISBN Number 0-9741760-6-0

Printed in the United States of America

Table of Contents

DEDICATION AND ACKNOWLEDGMENTS

As I write this, I feel like someone who has just won an Oscar®. There are so many people to thank and only so much time, or in this case, space, to do so.

With that said, I first thank my mother and father who influenced me every day just by being my parents. You are my parents, but you are also teachers and role models to each of your children and grandchildren. In a world that struggles with commitment, you have stayed together through all trials and remained the foundation of your children's belief in family.

Specifically, to my mom, who never complains: You have influenced thousands of students over your 35-year commitment to education, and you have influenced me to go for my dreams. You are more than a teacher; you are a role model to your students and family. To my dad: You moved to Houston and lived with five other families, and in one generation, all of your children have graduated from college. You inspire us all, and we are honored to make you proud of what you have sacrificed to give us opportunities and options we enjoy today. Thank you, Mom and Dad. I love you.

Although I could write a book on how much I appreciate my mother and father and sisters, I dedicate this book to my wife. Wendy, you have shown me what it is to live life by a standard. You have demonstrated that commitment, loyalty and trust can be given freely, because you would never live another way. Your consistency in loving me, even when I was more than unlovable, has encouraged me to be my best and live up to my potential. Your love for God and family has made me a better man, husband and father. When you had my ring made, the jeweler inscribed something for me to remember. I was looking at it just the other day and realized that true relationships are exactly as you inscribed: "Always and Forever"! You are my "Always and Forever," so thank you for all the little things you do that I never mention enough.

To my three children, Gabriella, Jacob and Jonah: Your father loves each of you very much, and I hope to be the same influence for you that my parents were for me. When I was a teenager trying to make right decisions, the thought always crossed my mind, "If I do this, will it make my parents proud of me?" I hope to have that same positive influence on each of you.

Special thanks to Dr. Robert Rohm, who has been a mentor and who taught me the DISC Model of Human Behavior. You have influenced me to take what I learned and apply it in my life. This information and your leadership have helped all of my relationships.

Special thank yous to Chris Carey and Rick Herceg. You believed in me enough to work on this project and allowed me to express my ideas and get them into print. I am forever grateful for the friendships and experience of this project.

To all my students at Kingwood High School, Kingwood Christian Academy, and Memorial High School: More than students, you have been my teachers. Keep dreaming, stretching and growing. Don't forget, you own your own company! Run it well.

To David Knight: Your belief in me and support of my dreams is beyond thanks, as if I were a part of your family. I cannot find words to describe what a generous and giving man you have been. For all the times you have given to others, I say thank you for all of them as well!

FOREWORD

Influencer Incorporated is a must-read for anyone who is serious about becoming a better leader, parent or spouse. Pete Hinojosa's storytelling provides a basis for looking at our own struggles in a way that is not condemning or judgmental. His style allows readers to feel comfortable in evaluating their current condition.

The use of the DISC method to determine what drives our desires and needs provides a solid platform to build on. Pete describes how each of us has innate tendencies in relationships, whether at work, home or socially. By using the DISC profile program, readers gain an in-depth understanding of their own profile, in addition to the profiles of business associates, friends and loved ones.

Pete provides readers with a basic "how-to" handbook for self-improvement and gives step-by-step procedures to unlock their potential. He begins by setting the reader up in business, quantifying the value of being an *Influencer* versus a *Controller.* He ties the common thread of business ownership throughout the book, validating why one should pursue the higher calling as an *Influencer.*

This book can be used by people in any profession or station in life. Pete provides a blend of real-life stories and quotes from famous leaders that maintains one's interest throughout.

As a leader of a large sales organization myself, I encourage our people to study the habits of successful leaders. One of the books I encourage them to read is Dale Carnegie's classic, *How to Win Friends and Influence People.* Written 70 years ago, it is a basic study of human relations. Pete's book picks up where Dale Carnegie leaves off. It will continue to be a must-read for years to come.

> — Jay Mincks
> Chief Operating Officer
> Administaff

PETE'S PREFACE

Before we get started officially, it might be helpful to know *why* you should read this book. I've been talking about the "Influencer Incorporated" idea for five years, and now it is in print. You've got it in your hands, and I think it will be different from anything else you've read.

The title comes from two really important ideas:
- **Influencer:** You really can choose to be an *Influencer* who makes a difference in the lives of others.
- **Incorporated:** You really work for yourself in life — you're your own company.

We're going to develop these two themes together, and when we've finished, our goal is to have you set you up for a profitable life. To do this, we'll look at you like any other business, including:
- Your product (that's you)
- Your prospective consumers (people you meet)
- Your assets and liabilities (what makes you unique)
- Your stock value (what you're worth to others who know you and invest in you)
- Your growth potential (how to keep your future value on the rise)

Two Relationship Choices

About this "influence" thing. It will become a real success key for you. You've seen people who are all about control. *Controllers* boss-and-leverage their way through life, clueless as they force people to do things their way. Mostly, *Controllers* get their own way by overlooking others and promoting themselves. While people may do their bidding, it happens with anger and resentment. *Controllers* brighten up a room when they leave!

Then there are people who are *Influencers*. They build teams that accomplish great things — and some people actually get excited about working with *Influencers*. They don't resent that they've "got to" do things — they appreciate that they "get to" do things with *Influencers*. It's possible to achieve much more through influence than *Controllers* could ever hope to accomplish. And, as you might guess, *Influencers* brighten rooms when they enter!

Together, we're going to look at *your* life (wherever you live it — work, home or school) and see how you can influence more and control less — and still be more effective with people than you ever imagined.

In My Prior Life

As we work through these concepts, you'll find that I didn't always think this way. Was I a control freak? I wouldn't have said so, but other people might have. I prefer to think I was just "influence-challenged."

My relationships throughout high school and college, could be described as one disaster chasing another. I was unfaithful and lacked the commitment to stick out the challenges of interacting with people. I always wanted to do well, but, no matter who I dated, we always ended badly. And then I would look back, sigh in disgust and confusion, and think, "There goes another year of my life." Getting together and breaking up became a destructive and predictable pattern.

Finally, I asked my dad how he *knew* my mom was the

woman for him. "How do you know who you're supposed to be with?" I asked. He replied, "Son, you need to find someone who trusts you more than you even trust yourself."

Although I was already 23 years old, I had no idea what he meant. I shrugged and said, "Okay, Dad." It was in my second year of teaching that I discovered what he was talking about. That's when I met a girl who changed my life. (Don't skip to another part of the book *now!* This is where it gets good — and it's going to be a vital part of the lesson.)

Love Is Where It Finds You

I was at a local tennis shop, waiting patiently while the owner helped a customer who was desperate to figure out how to get her racquet repaired and returned before leaving town. Another woman entered and engaged herself in their conversation. She took charge immediately — volunteered to bring the racquet herself when she played tennis later that night.

After she had solved that dilemma, she walked over to me, looked me in the eye and asked, "Are you married?" Before I could answer, she added, "Because I have daughter, and she would just love you!"

I was stunned. I said, "No, I'm not married and...." I hadn't finished when she continued. "What's your name?"

"Pete Hinojosa...."

"Well, I'm Betty and my daughter is Wendy. She is 5-foot-7, has blue eyes and blonde hair, and she is beautiful."

I decided to mess with her: "Do you have a picture of your daughter?"

"Oh sure," Betty replied — and she hurried out to her car to get her wallet, which was filled with pictures of this Wendy person from the time she was two until she was 22!

I agreed that Wendy was very pretty. Betty immediately corrected me: "She is not *pretty* — she is *beautiful!*"

I agreed, "Okay, she's *beautiful.*"

I asked where Wendy had gone to high school and college and found out she had attended the same high school I had, and had graduated from Texas Tech with her BS degree in Education.

My interest was piqued, but I played hard to get. I did everything I could to tell Betty I wasn't interested. With all the conviction I could muster, I said, "I appreciate the offer, but I am just a teacher — and it seems to me that you have a certain ideal standard for your daughter."

Betty shot back: "Son, money's not everything."

I said, "Give me her number."

I didn't want to seem desperate, so I waited till the next day to call. I gathered my courage, and when Wendy answered the phone, I explained that I'd met her mom, who said I should call. *Silence.*

Finally, she replied with a question I had never been asked at the start of a relationship: "Do you believe in God?" I felt awkward and tried to be funny: "You mean like on Sundays?" This was followed with more silence. I moved quickly to recover. "Oh, sure," I said, "I believe in God." Her question and my answer became the starting point of the best and biggest change of my life.

Wendy and I talked for hours on the phone, every day, all week, until I picked her up for our first date — we went to the Outback Steakhouse. I found that her personal integrity and spiritual life were so important to her that she wouldn't have even agreed to meet me if she hadn't sensed that I was looking for those things, too. Truth is, I didn't know where to find them, and she showed me the way. We were married six months later, and I haven't been the same person since!

She Never Said I Had To Change

It was a few years before I could put a name on what was so special about life with Wendy. When we were dating, so many little things about her surprised me.

I found few reasons to trust any girl I had dated previously, but I knew, almost immediately, that I could trust this one.

> **It wasn't as much *what* she said but *how* she said it — and more important, *how* she lived it.**

She just believed there was a right way to treat people and a wrong way. She was caring without being smothering. She was loving without being possessive. She wanted me to know how much I meant to her, but she never seemed jealous.

To test her out, I said maybe we were moving too fast — we barely new each other — so we should leave our options open. She responded like no other girl I'd ever dated. She said, "Fine," but her underlying tone said, "If you think you can find someone who will love you more and stay by your side through thick and thin, then go ahead!"

I went home a little confused but sure my "open options" suggestion was the dumbest thing I'd ever said. This woman was *different!* I had a stern talk with myself: "You, my friend, are going to change! Commit yourself to this relationship and to her. Or, play the 'Grass Is Greener Game' forever. You already know it never ends and you never win!"

I started noticing other things about my soon-to-be wife. She was loyal, she was kind, she cared about others and thought about how to be a good friend. Even to this day, the thought of offending or hurting someone on purpose fails to register with her.

I used detachment as my defense mechanism, but Wendy saw it for what it really was — a lack of trust. I had tons of acquaintances, while Wendy had a couple of really great friends. If I managed to talk with my friends once in a while, that was okay. But if she didn't truly connect with her friends regularly, she worried if they were all right. Wendy never told me what I should watch on TV, but I noticed she would leave the room if she felt it was inappropriate for her to watch.

(Now, before I go too far in cataloging all the virtues of Wendy, Queen of the Near-Perfect, I want you to know that my wife would be embarrassed if she knew I planned to tell you all this. Quite honestly, it's too much for almost anyone to live up to. But I'm telling you all this to help you see the *power* of the person of influence to make a difference in the lives of others. If she hadn't been so genuinely "that way" — not questioning or compromising her internal standard — I never would have felt prompted to take a closer look at so many areas of my own life.)

It seemed to me that whatever path Wendy had chosen was much brighter than mine. She walked it freely, with little to hamper her or cause her to stumble. I navigated my path cautiously, often tripping over my bad decisions and my constant need for control. She didn't see me as her "project" to fix. She really wasn't particularly aware of her influence on me — it was "unconscious influence," not "conscious control," that began making a difference.

Wendy understood the power of consistency.
She never sought to control me.
She simply expected more.
She simply lived it.
Wow!

This book is about you and me learning how to live a life of this kind of influence, too.

INFLUENCER INCORPORATED

Chapter 1:
WHAT A WEIRD TITLE FOR A BOOK!

For several years, I've been teaching an 18-week course on Student Leadership for high school juniors and seniors in Houston, Texas. The lessons are about seeing life with a different view. I'm glad I also have the opportunity to share these concepts, through business seminars, with adults who are out there competing in the workforce.

At the outset, it's important that you understand this book is in no way about "Pete Hinojosa, the Influencer." I didn't even set out to be one. Truthfully, I was teaching biology at a time when great things began happening in my life — and, as I shared them with my students, they began to discover that great things were happening in their own lives.

So this book shows how even thick-headed Pete was able to learn that influence is better than control. It's about recognizing a standard. We often don't recognize how far we've fallen into a negative pattern until we compare our actions to the original standard.

I've developed great respect for the young people who sit in my classroom. In significant ways, they are not my *students* but my *peers* because, together, we're exploring and discovering life. Our success isn't because I'm such a great teacher, but because the lessons we learn together in class provide a solid foundation on which to build their lives. This book puts into print some of the most important lessons of the class.

What It Means To Be An Influencer

The main themes involved in the *Influencer Incorporated* title are these:

- You are responsible for your own life and career advancement. Even if you have a job, understand that you really are self-employed by your own "company."
- Your "company" offers products and services. This means you need customers and, perhaps, investors.
- Loyal customers are developed by establishing mutually profitable relationships.
- You can choose between two business models, either "Controller Limited" or "Influencer Incorporated."
- The first model seeks success by pursuing self-interests and manipulating others for personal gain.
- The second model seeks success by pursuing mutual benefits with a sincere desire to help others.
- The first model operates through negative control of others.
- The second model operates through positive influence on others.

Unlike the business world, it's not *competition* against other *Influencers* that drives or determines the success of our efforts. After all, I can't force anyone to prefer my influence. Because of its quality, accessibility and consistency, people will choose it on their own. It's my influence, not my control, that brings people to see the standard I follow. In influence, people are drawn to character and repelled by the lack of it. The issue of character seems to be decided by how consistently I adhere to the standard.

Do I follow the standard without question, or do I follow the standard when it suits my self-interest?

Chapter 1: What A Weird Title For A Book!

Understand Your Brand

Controllers think their value can be established in "name *recognition*" when people know what their brand *is*. On the other hand, *Influencers* understand that their value is established with "name *appreciation*" when people know what their brand *means*. This is not just semantics or a game of words. The real deal is what people *think* about you and your character. When you *exert* control negatively over people, they think of you as selfish; when you *exercise* influence positively with people, they think of you as generous.

We see this name appreciation principle handled and mishandled in advertising all the time. The reason McDonald's has enjoyed a market-share preference over Burger King isn't because its food items are significantly tastier. From its founding, "Mickey-D" has intentionally pursued name *appreciation*. Surveys have shown that when consumers think of Burger King, they see it as "the Home of the Whopper" and the slogan, "Have it your way!" When consumers think about McDonald's, they consider "Ronald McDonald House" and its related children's charities, and they tend to think of it as "Your Kind of Place." Both brands are *recognized* for their product, but McDonald's has gained more *appreciation* in consumers' minds for services that are not visibly product-related.

My friend Chris Carey was a marketing advisor for McDonald's, and he explains it as a difference in how the name "tastes" when people say it: "Burger King? Oh yeah...." and "McDonald's? *Oh yeahhhh!*" It has nothing to do with food but with perception and reputation. It is built over time and can be lost very quickly. Which companies' reputations can you identify because of their positive or negative name *appreciation*? (*Hint:* you could start with Firestone, MCI, and Martha Stewart, and ask why.)

In marketing a product or service, companies develop their *Unique Selling Proposition* (USP) — what benefit can customers get from them that they can't get from another company? What makes them distinct and preferable in the customers' minds? Without a USP that has value to the consumer, where is their advantage?

So, when you think about *yourself* in company terms, the success of your brand name becomes very important. Your brand is how your customers think of you. What do they say? What are they "buying"? How's your quality control and your customer service? What's up with your commitment, consistency and reputation? Successful companies have repeat customers and good word-of-mouth. In similar ways, people will promote you as you run your life with character and positive principles.

Before we move on, complete your first assignment. It's on the next page and asks you to think about your own USP. Think about what you bring to people that satisfies their needs and enhances your value in their eyes — rather than evaluating what makes them useful to you.

Were you surprised that these questions involved both your professional and personal life? I think we need to be mindful of our brand in both "markets."

Some people love their work and hate coming home. Other people love coming home and hate going to work. Some people don't like either, and others love them both! What causes us to react in these ways? My conversations reveal that whether we love or hate these environments is closely connected to the quality of our relationships in them. It's been said that "People go where they are celebrated, not tolerated."

Let's think about your brand. Here's your first assignment. (If you were in a classroom, working for a grade, you wouldn't skip over this. Since you have a lot more at stake than just a grade, give this your best effort! I've included my own USP responses as a get-started example.)

- In my work life, what products and services do I offer?
  (For me: helpful relationship information.)

- Who are my customers, clients and investors?
  (For me: parents, teachers, teens, companies.)

- What unique value do I bring to the best of them?
  (For me: practical applications of quality information.)

- In my home life, what products and services do I offer?
  (For me: loyal, dedicated husband and father.)

- Who are my customers, clients and investors?
  (For me: my wife and children.)

- What unique value do I bring to the best of them?
  (For me: my love for them and my example.)

Don't you like being in places where you are not controlled and manipulated, but feel valuable and have influence? I think that feeling has a lot to do with how well we feel understood and appreciated.

In your work or family life, do you feel you live in influence? Do you feel that others you live and work with have a positive influence on you? Or do you feel restricted and trapped in either?

Do you feel your employer and family have your best interests at heart? Do they understand you? Or have your company or family overlooked and misunderstood you? Do they have a listening ear, or do they seem deaf to you and your needs?

Maybe you're happy with some aspects of your work and family life but not satisfied with others. There are probably people at your job you enjoy being around, but others make the whole experience painful. Perhaps it's the same for you at home — you relate better to some family members than others. You and your spouse are doing fine, but you struggle with your children. Or you're doing great with the kids but struggle with your spouse.

Paul Tournier, a Swiss physician and psychiatrist beautifully expressed the idea that our security in feeling loved and safe is tied to how well we feel understood and valued:

He who loves understands, and he who understands loves. One who feels understood feels loved, and one who feels loved feels sure of being understood.

We've all got needs, wants and expectations in our relationships. We do all kinds of things to meet and satisfy them, and it seems our efforts turn on the words *Control* and *Influence*. One of these is far better than the other, as we'll see.

Chapter 1: What A Weird Title For A Book!

The First Principle Of Influence

It is much better to have a positive effect on others than to have a negative effect. (I like to keep things simple! I've been told that football coach Vince Lombardi had a simple approach, too. At the beginning of every training camp, he began by explaining, "Boys, *this* is a football.")

So we begin with the first principle: You will have an effect on people, whether it is positive or negative overall. And it's better to have a positive than negative one.

As a parent (if you are one), you want to be a positive influence on your children, right? Don't you love it when your kids come back from an outing away from you, and another parent or teacher tells you they were well-behaved and represented you well?

Sometimes kids do things away from home that they wouldn't dare do under a parent's watchful eye. Can I give you an example? Hmmmm — how about school? Here's a common everyday interaction between many teachers and some students. We call it the "If it isn't for a grade, then forget any real effort" syndrome.

The teacher says: Here is your assignment for tonight.
The student thinks: You've got to be kidding. I already have other things to do.
The teacher says: Please type your assignment and turn it in tomorrow.
The student thinks: What excuse can I possibly make so I don't have to fire up the computer or do anything more than necessary?
The teacher says: Really put some effort into this assignment. I want to see that you took your time and really thought about it.

The student asks: Just how long does this paper have to be? (*The student thinks:* I'm not writing one word beyond the required assignment.)

The teacher says: Well, that's really up to you. I just want you to do a thorough job.

The student thinks: Good! I like vague instructions where I get to decide. This plays right into my philosophy of doing the minimum to get by. To me, "thorough" means a couple of sentences!

Are you getting the picture? As a teacher, I've noticed this alarming trend among students. What could be its cause? Drugs? Alcohol? (Please say it isn't *s-e-x!*) If high performance isn't required for a grade, or if students don't deem the assignment especially worthy, only a few go above and beyond to produce superior work.

Here's what's so frustrating to me about this scenario: I got into the teaching profession because I wanted to influence young minds, but sometimes I've left work feeling I was only a survivor in the battle for control.

And yes, sometimes I wonder what kind of influence I have on my children at home that makes them think this way. I've come to realize that they wear the family brand. My "little acorns" didn't fall far from the tree!

Maybe, as a parent, I wear a brand of excellence at work, but I let down at home, where I'm sometimes less like a leading brand and more like a bargain brand.

Sometimes it's at home that we do well, and for whatever reasons, we fail to be excellent at work. Don't you hate it when you hear a service provider, a coworker, or an employee give excuses? How about these:

That's not my job!
It's not my responsibility.
I just work here.
That's not my department!
You didn't tell me I was supposed to do that!
Well, I was absent — how was I supposed to know?
I don't remember your saying that!
No one told me about it!
I was really busy.
I had more important things to do.
What do you mean, how much time did I spend on this?
This is my best! How would you know what my best is?

Sure, you've heard them — have you ever used any of them? I've done both, on the job and at home. Our business and family lives intertwine.

If *your* boss gave you a project but you wanted to do something else, could you simply decide not to do it? Can you imagine, time after time, turning in your reports scribbled on a napkin? Or when assigned a project, you just blew it off? How long would it take to lose your job in the real world? Why don't students get that? Who's helping them establish *their* brand?

God knows how much a teacher can stand, so in kindness and wisdom, we are sometimes provided with a few students who arrive at school eager and prepared. They're easy to spot:

- *They* put a little extra effort into every assignment, no matter how trivial.
- *They* turn in homework on time.
- *Their* papers are not only well written and well researched, but legible.
- *They* even put their papers in plastic covers, just for the added excellence.

- *They* listen when they are supposed to and ask questions when they don't understand.
- If *they* are absent, *they* go to their teachers or take it upon themselves to get their assignments.
- They set high standards for all the other students!

I saw such a dramatic difference between these two types of students that I couldn't take it any longer. So I created an analogy they could understand. I told them that:

- Each owned their own company, called *Influencer Incorporated.*
- Every action, no matter how insignificant it seemed to them, represented a part of their company's image.
- Every time they interacted with people was important.
- Every time they spoke to others was important.
- Every time they made a promise or a commitment meant something.
- Every time they turned in a piece of paper, it was a representation of their company.
- They were to think about the impression they would leave on others in all areas of their lives.
- No longer were they to just get by. They were to push themselves to become an *Influencer* — a real, true, positive influence on others!

Now I am challenging *you* with the identical proposition. You own your own company, also called *Influencer Incorporated.* It is open for business *24/7.* You influence people, either positively or negatively. When people leave your company, they tell others about your products and customer service. They may recommend you to others or run down your brand, your value, and your stock, saying, in effect, "Trust me — their products and customer service aren't any good!"

Chapter 1: What A Weird Title For A Book!

Your company has at least two branch offices: one at work and one at home. What do both environments have in common? *Answer:* Your company's success depends on your skill in interacting with people at both locations.

Your Influence Perspective

Being a *Controller* doesn't require nearly the people skills of being an *Influencer.* But the rewards aren't as great either. A goal of this book is to provide you with a personality perspective, so you'll understand better:

- How people think
- Why they do the things they do
- How you can use this knowledge to lessen their control over you
- How you can use this knowledge to improve your influence with them
- How you can teach this information to others and help create a world of positive *Influencers*

What is your perspective about the world around you? How do you deal with the people in your life? Do you lead as an *Influencer,* or are you constantly seeking to be a *Controller*?

Can you see more than one perspective in any given situation? Which perspective is right? Which perspective, if any, is better for the situation? Which perspective is wrong? What if it's your perspective that's wrong?

How do you think you come across to others? Are you a positive *Influencer* or are you more a negative *Controller*? What lasting impression stays behind when you leave? Can simply understanding how you are being perceived, and how to more effectively work with others, change your environment at home and at work?

Would you like to *increase* your effectiveness at work and home? Would you like to *decrease* stress and *improve* communication in your key relationships? Would you like to see the people you love also live with less stress and more productivity?

Who is the one person at work you'd like to get along with better? Who's the one person at home you'd like to get along with better?

What project at work would you like to see come together more smoothly and efficiently? How would you like to see people around you respond more positively when you talk to them, and even when you ask for something to be done around the house?

Positive and affirmative answers to all of these questions — and more — await you as we dive into *Influencer Incorporated.*

Helpful Hints: In each chapter, consider the information for at least two separate applications:
- How you can use it to make your work environment better and more productive
- How you can use it to improve your family life and relationships.

Soon you'll experience increasing success in these two areas. And then you'll see your success broaden to include your spiritual life and your relationships with others. It will be exciting to watch your growth as you become an *Influencer.*

Chapter 2:
THE WAY YOU DO THE THINGS YOU DO

To be an effective and positive *Influencer*, it's important to understand and communicate with yourself and others. Each of us has identifiable — even predictable — preferences, attitudes, viewpoints and behaviors. These work together to form what people refer to as your personality style.

I regularly present this information to junior and senior high school students, who are able to put it to immediate use. So you needn't be a psychologist to grasp the concepts. You will quickly recognize applications for your own life experience and probably will be amazed that you weren't taught these valuable insights in your own school *daze* — make that *days!*

Before we get into explanations, you've got an assignment to complete. It's really important that you do it so you have a frame of reference for this information. You're going to create a personality profile for your own behavioral style. Since this book's pages are valuable "real estate," the accompanying CD contains a Personality Style Survey you can print out and complete. Its results will help you understand your Pace and Priority, the two factors that influence so much of how you see life and what you do in your environment.

COMPLETE THE SURVEY NOW....then return to this chapter to begin applying it!

Measuring Human Behavior

Did you complete your assignment already? Actually, depending on your personality style, even the answer to this question is predictable!

- Some readers dutifully did as instructed — they want to be cooperative and meet expectations.
- Other readers couldn't be bothered with what seemed like a detour — they just wanted the bottom line.
- Others wanted to be thorough and follow directions to the letter — but they bogged down in trying to see the pattern and second-guess the outcome.
- Some began it, got distracted and ran out of time — they shrugged it off and ended up reading these words.

So, if you haven't completed your assignment, this is a great time to do it. Where did you put that CD?

If you have completed the Personality Style Survey, you've created a graph that reveals the intensity of **D**, **I**, **S** and **C** characteristics and traits in your makeup — whatever *they* are! You'll find out what they are in this chapter.

When we say "personality," we're focusing on a pattern of behavior. There's much more the word *can* mean, but for the sake of our discussion, we'll use "personality style" and "behavioral style" interchangeably. There are four basic personality types, and they can combine together in various ways to make individual personality styles. Here's a really brief overview of how human behavior works. It's worthwhile for you to understand it because you'll learn how different people view their world and prefer to be engaged. Your key will be knowing how to interpret their observable behaviors.

The first factor we'll consider is whether you tend to be *active* and *outgoing* or *passive* and *reserved.* These opposites are shown in this circle representing *Pace.*

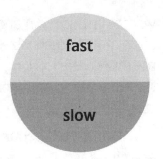

Faster-paced people are always on the go. If we compare *Pace* to a motor, they would be racing their engines and going as fast as they can. They like going and doing, not sitting and waiting. They tend to be:

- Active, Outgoing
- Action-Oriented
- Energetic
- Unstructured

The opposite *Pace* is *slower-paced.* If we use the motor analogy again, these folks tend to ride the brake and take their time. They don't need activity to recharge their batteries. They tend to be:

- Passive
- Less Active
- Reserved
- Structured

To avoid possible confusion early on, **DISC** is not designed to measure whether someone is "extroverted" or "introverted" in psychological terms. While the **DISC** theory is psychologically sound, it examines how to understand observable behaviors rather than diagnose psychological states. But if thinking in terms of "active, outgoing, extroverted" explains *faster-paced* to you, okay. Likewise, a *slower-paced* person need not be "passive, reserved, introverted" in strict psychological terms, but you can think of similar words to describe how they behave.

To help you visualize the *Pace* concept, break up the words "active" and "outgoing" and "passive" and "reserved." *Faster-paced* people need to *act, act out, go out,* and just be *on the go.* They want to be *out, not in,* and *on the go, not sitting still.* They make the most out of situations with their energy and enthusiasm. But if they stay there too long, they want to be *on the go* again! When they hear the magic words, "Would *you* like to *go...*", they don't care about any other detail — they just want to *go!*

Faster-paced people talk fast, eat fast and want to do everything fast. They are energetic in dealing with situations. They become actively involved and are not passive about what is important to them at the time. They don't want to miss out on something good. "Expectant" is a good word — they tend to make things happen and look for their desired outcome. They begin with enthusiasm. "Restless" describes them, too, since they like to be involved in new and different experiences.

What about people who have a more passive and reserved pace? "Pass" and "serve" are words we can break out to describe them. They tend not to be early adopters, so when something new comes along or change is introduced, their predictable response is usually "I'll pass." Once there is a track record, they may reconsider, but they need to take their time. Because of their tempo, they tend to work in the background, so "serve" describes them well, too. *Faster-paced* people tend to start with enthusiasm, but then lose interest. *Slower-paced* people tend to operate over the long term, so sometimes they are the only ones left when *faster-paced* people move on. In response to "Would you like to *go*" questions, they have their own: "Where are we going?" "Who's going with us?" "Why are we going and how long will we be there?" "How much money do we need?" "When are we coming back?" They are tortoises; active, outgoing people are hares.

Slower-paced people need to take their time and not be rushed. They prefer to stop, look and listen before jumping into situations and react with stress when pressured to act quickly. This *Pace* allows them to think about outcomes before jumping in. You can see this tendency when they drive — they are more likely to brake for yellow traffic signals!

How fast does your internal motor like to run? Are you a pedal-to-the-metal person or do you tend to ride the brake? You've heard of RPMs — at how many revolutions per minute the engine runs. If your *Pace* is fast, you operate in *Rapid* Personality Mode — high RPMs! If your *Pace* is slow, you operate in *Reserved* Personality Mode — lower RPMs!

The other consideration in your behavioral style is *Priority*. People tend to be either *task-oriented* or *people-oriented*. These opposites are shown in this circle, which represents *Priority*:

Task-oriented people are more drawn to projects and achievements. If we compare *Priority* to a steering wheel, they steer toward accomplishing goals and getting things done. If we look for their "true north," we'll find their compass points toward getting the job done and away from people. Using their time with specific outcomes in mind, they tend to be:

- Achievement-Oriented
- Purposeful
- Results-driven
- Focused

People-oriented folks seem more interested in the human drama. They naturally steer toward spending time with others and being involved in their lives. They like social interaction and tend to use their time to connect with people. Their "true north" points them toward people, and they may find more fulfillment in relationships than achievements. They tend to be:

- Relational
- Adaptable

- Warm
- Friendly

When we overlap these two half-circle diagrams, we come up with a four-quadrant diagram that illustrates the basic behavioral styles:

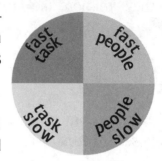

- Faster-paced / task-oriented
- Faster-paced / people-oriented
- Slower-paced / people-oriented
- Slower-paced / task-oriented

These easily observable differences in *Pace* and *Priority* create an impact that is far more profound than you might expect at first glance. In fact, many people overlook these factors because they seem so basic and simple. What is really interesting to me is that this behavioral model allows us to *predict* how people will respond to us and to what's happening. This provides opportunities to think through our interactions so we can adapt and adjust our expectations and behaviors to work more smoothly with others.

The Model Of Human Behavior

Remember the letters **D**, **I**, **S** and **C** in your graph? Since we've laid out the basic theory, now we can add these letters and gain an observable, predictable understanding of how people behave. Check out what the letters stand for:

D stands for *Dominance*. Researchers discovered that people who are *fast-paced* and *task-oriented* see their world as a challenging environment that must be controlled. They use phrases like "Hurry Up!" and "Let's Go!" Conflict gives them an opportunity to show what they're made of, and they tend to be very competitive. They see themselves as winners and like to win decisively. Most **D**s don't know when to quit. They get down to business and tend to be enthusiastic about their latest projects. They prefer to see the big picture instead of dealing with small details. They delegate work they don't like, but still want to be in charge of making high-impact decisions.

Here are some **D** words that describe their observable and predictable behaviors:

- Dominant
- Direct
- Decisive
- Dictatorial
- Dreamer

- Demanding
- Determined
- Doer
- Dogmatic
- Defiant (opposes rules)

I stands for *Influence* in the original **DISC** research, but the meaning of the word is different. *Faster-pace* and *people-oriented* individuals see the world as a friendly environment that must be celebrated. They really work for participation and are naturally fun and friendly. They use verbal skills to persuade others. (This is what the researchers meant by "influence," although sometimes it can seem more like manipulation. It's an important distinction, as you'll see while working your way through this information.) *Interacting* is another word that demonstrates how they relate to people. No one is a stranger to them. They hate being alone and need the approval and acceptance of friends, companions and buddies. **I**s tend to be emotional and excitable, wearing their hearts on their sleeves. They like variety and "high-touch" activities, and want to avoid repetitive, predictable jobs isolated from people.

Here are some **I** words that describe their observable and predictable behaviors:

- Imaginative
- Impressive
- Impressionable
- Interchangeable
- Impulsive
- Inducing
- Interesting
- Important
- Interested in people
- Illogical (a "feeler")

S stands for *Steadiness*. Researchers discovered that people who are *slower-paced* and *people-oriented* see their world as a friendly environment that must be included rather than shut out. They seek harmony and agreement, and they tend to be good listeners. They will shut down when conflict threatens, rather than oppose publicly. They prefer to work on one project at a time and like closure before moving on to something else. People operating in this style thrive when you appreciate them for who they are. Public recognition isn't usually necessary, but letting them know how much they are valued is important. Two-way trust and communication enable them to feel secure.

Here are some **S** words that describe their observable and predictable behaviors:

- Supportive
- Specializing
- Sweet
- Shy
- Sentimental
- Stable
- Servant
- Submissive
- Status Quo
- Sucker (can't say no)

C stands for *Compliance*. Researchers discovered that people who are *slower-paced* and *task-oriented* see the world as a challenging environment that must be corrected. They care a great deal about accuracy and rely on facts and logic rather than opinion and emotion. They want to take their time and be consistent in their actions. They know to double-check things and look deeper than the surface. Often, they have the ability to solve problems well and can possess great insight into life because they ask "why" questions. "Because" is never a sufficient answer; they keep digging until they find the reason behind the reason.

Here are some **C** words that describe their observable and predictable behaviors:

- Competent
- Cautious
- Critical Thinking
- Compliance Seeking
- Correct

- Cognitive
- Consistent
- Conformist
- Conscientious
- Cold (unfriendly)

Each type has a different perspective. Each sees the world through a different filter. Because most people have not been taught to understand and value these differences, they don't know how to appreciate each other's natural skills and contributions. As part of a team, they offer insights and protection to each other, but until we see how we can "fit" together, we try to eliminate what is different.

This diagram shows that **D** and **I** types are different in their *Priority,* although they have common ground in their *Pace.* **I** and **S** types are different in *Pace,* but they share the *Priority* of being people-oriented. **S** and **C** types focus on a different *Pri-*  *ority,* but both prefer a slower *Pace.* Both **C** and **D** types have a "get it done" *Priority,* although the *Pace* that is comfortable for them is different.

All of this means that there are areas in which the style of one individual will *naturally* be more comfortable working with others and areas where they will not. When differences are pronounced, some give-and-take adapting and adjusting is necessary in order to work together.

In these diagrams, you can see that there is no natural common ground between **D** and **S** types. They are opposite in both their *Pace* and *Priority*. The same is true for **I** and **C** types. When one wants to work faster, the other needs to work slower. When one is focused on achieving tasks, the other concentrates on building relationships. When opposites learn to respect, and benefit from, each other's viewpoints, the outcome can improve dramatically — such teams fill in each other's blind spots. For instance, **D** types tend to be enthusiastic as they start projects but **S** types' steadiness allow them to be solid finishers. **I** types can inspire others to handle changes well and **C** types may pay more attention to the details that make change happen smoother and more efficiently.

It might surprise you to know that these contrasting types can occur in an individual, too. As you might expect, such a personality style *blend* can cause internal conflicts. But at the same time, when people understand that even these are predictable, they are able to take advantage of their strengths and minimize the impact of their struggles.

Chapter 3:
THE PERSONALITY PERSPECTIVE

"Personality Perspective" refers to the **D**, **I**, **S** and **C** filters through which we see the world *and* the world sees us! No one else can truly know the exact motivations behind your actions and attitudes. Instead, people attach moral values to what they see you do, usually without understanding anything about personality styles and how they influence behavior. The goal of this chapter is to give you a handle on the four basic types so you can identify and understand them when you see them in action.

As high school juniors and seniors, most of my students want to understand how life and relationships work. Some approach this personality topic eagerly, seeking to know themselves and others better. Other students are defensive, resenting that such "personal" information is so readily available. A few hope that personality perspectives will give them power to manipulate people. One or two may see their "prewiring" as justification for offensive actions and attitudes.

Our goal is not just to *discuss* but to *act*, first understanding ourselves, then others, and finally adapting and adjusting to work and live cooperatively and successfully. So my classes can get maximum benefit, I give them a taste of how it works and then ask them to answer the question: "Why learn **DISC**?"

The following reply came from a student who wanted to communicate better with her dad. When she was little, she loved feeling safe and secure in his lap. "It's like Superman dropped me in mid-air," she told me. She once felt safe and secure in her relationship with her father, but now said, "I feel he never even noticed and let me flail until I hit the ground." She wanted to learn about **DISC** so she could relate to his style and they could talk again without his blowing up.

Although I usually don't argue with most people, my dad and I almost ALWAYS end up in an argument. Our personalities, viewpoints, and how we communicate with each other clash horribly. Whenever I try to tell him about something like grades, how I feel, problems or issues I have, we always end up butting heads and the whole point of what was trying (to be) communicated/accomplished is lost.

I still love my dad, but this puts HUGE stress in our relationship. I believe that if I begin to understand my own personality tendencies, preferences (etc.) I can then channel those things or calm them down in a way that could be "compatible" with my dad's personality.

This way, we will be able to communicate, get things done, get along better ☺ and just TALK!!! I hope learning this will enrich my relationship with my dad and get rid of a lot of unnecessary stress in our lives.

Throughout her senior year, she struggled and progressed, applying what she learned to build a stronger relationship with her father. Knowing this information isn't an automatic fix for conflicts, but I am always amazed at what it can do.

I wish I had known about the personality perspective as a high school student. You'll learn that I had a stormy relationship with my dad during this period of my life — we learned about personality types together at a conference after I began teaching school and had students of my own.

Debate, Discussion Or Argument?

Understanding personality perspectives would have helped the early years of my marriage, too. Many husbands and wives are attracted to the differences in their spouses *before* they marry and then set about "fixing" them afterward. I'm going to give you a real-life Wendy and Pete example, and if you have been married longer than ten minutes, you've probably experienced this phenomenon, too.

Wendy and I have different personality styles, so we naturally have different viewpoints about "debating." When I'm in a discussion about *anything*, I love to fight it out all the way to the end. However, unlike many who argue, when it's over, it's over — I don't spend a lot of time feeling bad or mad. I really enjoy the whole push-and-pull of such events. So it's not surprising that I've always thought there should be a clear-cut winner and loser in any debate. I don't really care *why* we are debating or *what* the debate is about. It's just really important for debaters to be fully engaged.

This worked well when it was just me and a bunch of guys debating sports teams, but it didn't work at all with Wendy. The more I tried to make my point, the more it seemed like a me-against-her confrontation, and I really hurt her feelings. You see, whenever this occurred at home, I called our debates "discussions" and Wendy called them "arguments."

How we "discussed" issues is much easier for me to explain when an audience can read my body language and understand my tone. I can *say* it more easily than *write* it — and I'll confess up front that I'm not proud of either my responses or results when I used this approach with Wendy. I'm swallowing my pride and sharing it with you because I think this one growth moment was the genesis of my understanding the difference between being an *Influencer* and a *Controller*, and why it was important for me to control *myself* rather than control others.

As far as I was concerned, I had typical **D** and **I** style "discussions" with Wendy, but they were "arguments" to someone like her with an **S** style. I can't even remember what topic was involved. In any case, I tried to make her feel that her point was invalid while mine was the only right view. For us, such "discussions" always ended in one of two ways:

- Wendy would become really quiet and not say anything at all. This is incredibly irritating to someone who wants to argue more. It quickly stops an argument when only one person engages. I shared this lesson with a lawyer friend who wants his firm's younger attorneys to learn this tactic. When someone tries to pull you off-focus, remain steady and calm. Don't engage in nonsense.
- Wendy would end up in tears. You're probably thinking, "Shame on Mean Pete for making Sweet Wendy cry," and you're right. I'm ashamed that I pushed her

so far to win dumb arguments. It's also worth noting that, no matter how many times this happened, she never once responded as I hoped when I said, "Stop crying!" It didn't work then and it wouldn't work now.

So this time, as our discussion/argument was going back and forth, I said too much. First came Phase One: she went silent. I really pushed to get her re-engaged. Wendy was teaching second grade, so I said, "A *third grader* could answer that question!" (This is usually the spot in my seminar when women groan and men wince. I told you I'm not proud of this!)

Well, Wendy just stood there. Then she etched something forever in my heart and mind as she asked, "Do you want to know why I don't always answer you when you say things like that to me?"

I thought, "I'm ready for this. Bring it on!"

She said, "I don't always answer you because I actually think about what I'm going to say and if I'm going to hurt your feelings." (Can't you hear the audience groaning and wincing again?)

In that moment, I saw myself as others frequently saw me. It was time to take a closer look at Pete, time to stop running and start learning. In one sentence, Wendy allowed me to see myself from a perspective that was selfish and prideful. I knew it was time to change!

I've told this story many times, and it never gets easier to explain that I cared more about winning that debate than I cared about hurting my wife's feelings. I began to see that influence is about seeing ourselves for who we really are and then, one step at a time, changing to become better.

Isn't it obvious that I had become very comfortable in my **D** and **I** pattern — saying what I thought in order to win? It's not the only *Controller* pattern, but it worked for me and my style. I was all about *my* point of view, *my* desires, *my* needs, *my* ego, and *my* unwillingness to see from my wife's viewpoint. It's not that **S** types, like Wendy, are always positive *Influencers*, but they do try to support people, bring peace and give a nonoffending response — good traits for anyone who wants to establish trust and build influence.

Think about what Wendy said and realize what it means to be an *Influencer.* She was thinking about what she said and how it might affect me. As she thought about me and acted on my behalf, she benefited, too — once I decided to get on board.

Even though she could have been as rude and obnoxious as I had been to her, she held to her high, consistent standard. She continued to do the right things, even when I would not. I thank God for the opportunity to change my approach and give her the respect she so freely gave me even then.

Here's another example from our everyday lives: I love to go and do. It doesn't take much to talk me into going out, and it's even easier if food is involved. Since my wife and I both teach, we like to jump into the car on Friday nights and head to eat.

Rather than deciding on my own, I've learned to temper my **D** decision-making reflexes and ask Wendy first where she would like to eat. We have three favorite restaurants in our neighborhood and I know she'll pick one of them, so I ask, "Honey, where would you like to go?"

She answers, "I really don't have a preference; you just decide for us." Bless her high-**S** heart! I name my favorite: "How about Mencius?" (For four years, I ordered the same thing every time we went there. Five years ago, I switched to something else. I've got my eye on a third dish now!) Wendy puts her hands on her hips, tilts her head, and makes that little noise that says she's really thinking it over. "Ummm, I'm not really in the mood for Chinese."

So I ask, "What are you in the mood for?" I think to myself that we have just two options left. She replies, "I don't know; you just decide for us." I think again that I had already decided but it didn't work. So I suggest, "How about Pasta Company?"

She thinks about it again and says, "I don't think I want lasagna." My **D** wants to advise, "Then don't get the lasagna — they have more than lasagna!" But there's no use in saying it because she always orders lasagna at Pasta Company. We move on to our final choice. I "synthesize" **S** and say, "Honey, how about if you just tell me where you want to go and we'll just go?"

She says, "Really, I don't have anything particular in mind — let's just go out and enjoy ourselves. Whatever you decide is fine with me." I had decided, not once but twice! But I don't fuss because, if I did, we wouldn't go out at all.

I announce "my" final choice with certainty. This is it, the old standby, the one that never fails — where we went on our first date: "Let's just go to Outback!" She stops, looks up, goes through how it feels to her. The suspense is killing me! Then the words I've been waiting for: "Yeah, that sounds really good." I head to the door, hearing her muse, "But you know how busy they get on Friday night, and it's so expensive...."

I say the only thing left to say: "Just get in the car!" It's not a difference between men and women. It's our styles. Sound familiar? If so, you married your opposite, too!

Arthur Gordon, author of *A Touch of Wonder*, wrote, "Nothing in life is more exciting and rewarding than the sudden flash of insight that leaves you a changed person — not only changed, but for the better." Thank you, Wendy, for giving me that opportunity.

Four Distinct Personality Types

My point is that each of the four types has a style of behavior that is comfortable for them, but the quirks of each type tend to make others uncomfortable.

Without a way of describing and understanding these differences, it's difficult for most people to accommodate them. Once we know what to look for, behaviors jump out at us everywhere we go, and we know what's happening.

Since much of my professional life has taken place in a classroom setting, let me give you an example. As I do, see if you can figure out the personality types likely being exhibited by my students:

I was lecturing a Biology class on cell structure and pulled down the overhead screen. To my surprise the screen made an unfamiliar "sprung spring" sound and wouldn't stay down. As soon as I let go, it rolled back up. I tried several times, using every teacher trick in the book to keep the screen down: pulling it out a little at a time, stopping every few inches, pulling it all the way out at once and jiggling it. Finally I made the obvious diagnosis to my class: "I think the screen is broken."

One student jumped up and was on his way even before he had finished saying, "You're not doing it right. Let me do it!" He grabbed it, pulled it up and down, jiggled it and tried everything except beating it with a hammer. Then he looked back at me and said, "Uh, Mr. Hinojosa, I think the screen is broken." I thought to myself, "No kidding? Thanks for your assistance!"

In response, another student pumped arms and fists into the air, shouting, "All right! Free day!" High-fives were exchanged among a group of party animals who had instantly lost track of the day's agenda. I started getting nervous, and an immediate build-up of panic sweat appeared on my shirt and brow. I thought to myself, "I'd better do something — fast!"

Another student raised his hand and protested, "Let me get this straight. This is third period, right? Did the first two periods get the notes?" I said they did. "Well, I can't get behind the other classes, so you're going to have to figure something out." That's when yet another student suggested, "Mr. H, why don't you just write it on the board? I don't want to get behind, either." Cool and objective, she presented a solution and refocused all of us on completing the task at hand. And I wondered, "Why didn't I think of that?"

One of my students said nothing until the class had ended, and then approached me at the door. "Mr. H, it's okay — we all have bad days. I think you recovered great! See you tomorrow."

Did you identify the four types? My "let me handle this" student was a forceful **D**. The easily distracted "school's out" student was an **I**. Then I threw you a curve: the "sensible solution" student was a **C**, evaluating and recommending. The last student was an **S**, strong on encouragement and sensitive to the emotions of others.

When I first started teaching, I had no idea where comments like these were coming from. I recognized that students acted and reacted differently in all situations. There is no such thing as "kids today" when describing their actions and attitudes. It wasn't until I learned about personality types that I began to appreciate the predictable differences I saw in my classroom.

Some kids struggle in relating their studies to their "real" lives. What may seem obvious from our frame of reference may not connect with them until they can relate to it on their terms. Students don't do things *against* their teachers; they are normally just doing things *for* themselves! (Just as "regular people" don't do things against you but for themselves.) Here's an example — in order to really enjoy it, see it from the perspective of a new teacher (*me*) who had no idea that people have predictable differences!

I often wondered what certain students were thinking when they spoke up. When I started teaching, I thought students were trying to sabotage my class. No matter what I did to make my lessons fun, it seemed certain students could, in one sentence or one action, destroy the flow in any lesson.

"I wrecked my truck!" Todd announced.

"I'm sorry, what did you say?" I asked incredulously.

"I wrecked my truck this weekend."

In this Biology class, we were supposed to be studying the difference between *biotic* and *abiotic* states. (The short and simple definition is that "biotic" describes living things, while "abiotic" describes a nonliving thing, like water, rocks, and mud).

When I said "mud," Todd could no longer contain his enthusiasm for the incredible distinction between *biotic* and *abiotic,* and his hand shot up — with purpose! The kind of purpose that teachers recognize immediately and think, "All right! This student is about to add something truly significant to the discussion!" Instead, he blurted, "I wrecked my truck!" I stopped, sucked in a deep breath, and asked, "*What?*" And he repeated, "Yeah, I wrecked my truck," and continued his tale to connect the dots for the rest of the class: "Me and my friends were out in my truck this weekend, and we went 'off-roading' and got stuck in the mud!"

Aha! The way he had made the abstract-science-to-real-world connection was brilliant: abiotic, friends, weekend, truck, wrecked, mud! I had cracked the code: Subtract *abiotic* and you're left with everything else Todd really wanted to talk about. He was just waiting for me to take a breath so he could sneak in his story and get a little recognition!

Actually, as an impulsive **I** who processes new information by talking about it, Todd had just discovered a way to relate to the lesson. It made sense to him and he was sharing it to be helpful, not disruptive. I'm glad I didn't follow my natural tendency and kick him out of class. I've discovered that the rules of typical classroom environments suit **S** and **C** students more comfortably than **D** and **I** students: be quiet, raise your hand, listen carefully, work as a team, solve problems systematically, pay attention to details and facts.

Again, when I first started teaching, I didn't understand how personality styles worked, but I learned that many of my students had tendencies that clashed with my own teaching style. There were four perspectives to be aware of:

- Certain students always wanted to be in charge and take the class away from me. If there were opportunities to lead, they were first to do so. They would normally question my ability and authority: "Are you sure you're a certified teacher?"

- Others wanted to monopolize class time with their stories and need for recognition. They would laugh loudly, get sidetracked very easily, and say things like, "That was funny, Mr. Hinojosa, but listen — this story's even better!"

- Still others were peacemakers. They just wanted everyone to get along and stay on track with no surprises. When I lost control, I could count on them to rescue me with, "Come on, you guys — give Mr. H a break!"

- Finally, some students questioned the validity of every statement or asked for in-depth information I wasn't always prepared to supply. "Are you sure that's right, Mr. Hinojosa? Why is that? What would happen if...?"

Once I learned about personality styles, I noticed that my students were acting and reacting according to predictable patterns. They weren't really out to get me! They were simply relating to my lessons through their perspective — their personality's point of view. It's like the fourth grader whose teacher asked him, "What would you have if you mowed 16 lawns and were paid $15 per lawn?" The boy thought for a moment and answered, "A brand-new bike!"

We usually think about our own point of view and basic needs. We connect with others only when we learn how to take our eyes off our perspective long enough to see their point of view.

When we don't always get the response we expect, my friend Chris Carey reminds us:

It's better to *complete* than *compete* with each other.

Students are concerned about how they appear, and they want to be appreciated for their unique assets, not criticized for supposed liabilities, like being outgoing or asking lots of questions. They want to be understood, and they're self-conscious about how they are perceived by peers.

Youth worker and author Ethel Barrett wrote, "We would worry less about what others think about us if we realized how seldom they do." As a teacher, my job is to think well, and often, about my students, connecting with each to the best of my ability, and to help them feel understood.

I've also noticed that students start each school year with a strange mix of excitement and anxiety:

"Who are your teachers?"

"Who do you have for Math, English, and Science?"

"What — you have him? He's really hard!"

"Oh, no! You have her? She fails everybody!"

"Yeah, my sister had her, and she's really easy."

Every so often, you may hear, "Oh, you're so lucky — that teacher is great!" Over the years, I've decided that what makes an ordinary teacher extraordinary is that little bit extra! The way they do their jobs and relate to their "customers" has built them a respected brand name. I wanted that brand, and my first years of teaching were a great learning experience in how to, and how not to, work with students.

In my second year, I was fortunate enough to see a remarkable person speak on personality styles. Dr. Robert Rohm unlocked the secrets of understanding behavior for me, and I wondered why I had not been introduced to these ideas in college, or even earlier.

As Dr. Rohm explained personality types, I feverishly tried

to take notes while laughing at our foibles and behaviors until I was almost out of breath. I was so impressed that I bought everything I could find on this topic. It was exactly what I was looking for — that little bit extra! I began putting what I was learning into action in my classroom immediately.

Earl Nightingale said, "If you'll spend an hour a day for five years on any given subject, you will become an expert in that subject." Now, eight years later, I've been certified as a human behavior consultant, making constant application of **DISC** behavioral principles with students, parents, teachers, couples, business leaders and my own family.

A Safe Place To Learn

Now, on the first day of class, I take some time to learn the name and something personal about each student. This helps them know that I think of them as *people,* not as *projects.* Behind me, on the board is some Japanese writing:

聞くは一時の恥じ、
　知らざるは一生の恥じ。

Kiku wa ittoki no haji,
Shirazaru wa issho no haji

Sometime during the first ten minutes of class, curiosity overwhelms at least one of my students, and he or she asks what the symbols mean. I explain two reasons for what I've written. First, as a science teacher, I am introducing them to the Scientific Method: observe, then state the problem. Second, the Japanese writing is a proverb: "To ask is but a moment's shame. Not to ask and remain ignorant is a lifelong shame."

I want my students to realize that the primary reason they are in school is to learn. Above all, I want them to feel confident for at least the one hour a day they are in my classroom. They can ask questions without feeling stupid or scared. They can act and feel like themselves, without the added pressure of worrying about what others think of them, especially their peers. Each is uniquely talented, and if I can help them understand this better while learning the required subject matter, I am doing my job.

> **When people feel accepted and safe and can be themselves, they always produce better results.**

Not Right Or Wrong, Just Different

One of my **DISC** mentors is Ken Voges. I attended a seminar where he talked about conflict resolution and personality differences. Having a lot of **I** in my own style, I liked to talk when Ken asked us questions. Being equally strong in **D** traits, I always thought I had the right answer.

> **Your personality style is a blend of D, I, S and C traits, not just one type. Different people are "high" in one and "low" in another. The variations are almost infinite, so one D can be quite different from another, depending on the blend of other traits that support the D. The same is true of the other types. A validated assessment tool can actually reveal the ratio of D, I, S and C in your individual style.**

At Ken's seminar, I was sitting next to someone who viewed life through **S** lenses, quite a contrast from my **D** and **I** perspective. She answered the same questions from a totally different viewpoint, and we didn't think alike at all. I wondered,

"Why would she say that? I would never handle the situation that way." Of course, no matter what I said, she disagreed. "I can't be thinking wrong on everything," I reasoned, "but she can't be wrong all the time, either."

That seminar was a turning point in my life. For the first time, I really understood that "different" was not always "wrong." It *could* just be different.

When I first began athletic coaching, my approach was determined by my **D** tendencies — my motivational techniques relied on competitiveness and aggression. I could intimidate my players easily, but I learned it takes the **I** trait of inspiration, the **S** trait of empathy and the **C** trait of strategizing to build a real team. I was *competing* against my players instead of *completing* them.

It's difficult to motivate people without catering to their needs — teaching and coaching according to their style, not just your own. I tell parents, "It's not a child's responsibility to learn your personality or mine; it's our responsibility to learn theirs." As mature adults, we need to accept our obligation to adjust to others. As we do this more accurately and consistently, our ability to communicate with others will improve noticeably.

Chapter 4:
Let's Face It!

In the last chapter, I mentioned briefly that no one is purely a **D**, **I**, **S** or **C** — these are the four basic behavioral types, but your own "personality style" is a blend of all four types. The ways these traits play out in our behaviors (along with our different motivating values, attitudes, experiences and interests) explain why someone can be recognized as a **D** (for instance) but not behave as another **D** you might know.

It's also true that you may behave like one style on the job because that's what your work demands, yet have a different style when you're off duty. No, you don't have a split personality! You have one natural, specific, recognizable, predictable behavioral style — the "real" you — but you can adapt and adjust your style temporarily in an effort to meet others' expectations or to be more successful in certain relationships. This will help you be a more effective *Influencer* and achieve the successful results that *Controllers* can only dream about!

If you are the parent of an **S** child and your personality style differs, it's inevitable that conflicts will arise. For example, if you have **D**-style expectations and discipline, you'll expect more and you'll push to get it:

- "Come on — you can do it!"
- "Try harder — don't you know winning is everything?"

Remember, to your slower-paced, conflict-avoiding, supportive son or daughter, winning may be much farther down on the list. After all, your compasses point in opposite directions, and your motors are tuned for different speeds.

If you're an **I** parent of an **S** child, you're going to be more excitable and active, and the **S** is more likely to be your cheerleader on the side, giving you encouraging comments and appreciation. Both of your compasses point toward people, but the pace of your motors are not the same.

If you are a strong **C** and are parenting an **S**, you are very task-oriented and your child is noticeably more people-oriented. As a result, differences will always arise in your compass, even while your motors may agree.

One of my students wrote an essay about her task-oriented mom, who makes lists for everything. She has separate lists for each possible excursion or vacation they might take — one for going to the beach, one for ski trips, one for picnics, one for an overnight stay, and so on — all filed on a computer. When she's preparing for a trip, she just pulls up the appropriate file and prints out her list.

It's not right or wrong, good or bad; it's just the way she likes to do it. On the list are items to pack and boxes to be checked off as each item goes into the suitcase. Everything that's on the list is a must, and whatever is packed should be on the list. The mom hands the list to her daughter and tells her to get to work.

As you might suspect, the daughter is *less* task-oriented and *more* people-oriented. She's still trying to find her suitcase and has no clue where she saw it last! They haven't even left home and she's wondering, "Are we going to have fun at all on this trip? We haven't even started, and already I'm unhappy!"

This is real life. It's a parent. It's a child. Or a husband. Or a wife. When they try to do "normal stuff" with each other, their natural preferences and predictable differences can create a response like, "I love you and I'm trying to understand you...but sometimes, I can't stand you!"

Here are some other ways differing styles may conflict with each other:

Cs often come across as too critical or strict because they want tasks done following certain procedures. **D**s may conflict on following procedures because they tend to care more about getting to the end result. **S**s tend not to initiate or innovate. They want to meet expectations but often wait for specific instructions. **I**s don't like routine, so if they have to do things over and over again, they try to make it fun and may miss some of the details. As you can see, there are differences in how each approaches a task.

A **D** may say, "We have a task to do, and you'd better do it right because I will be watching you!" A **C** may say, "We have a task to do, and if it 's going to be done right, I'll have to do it myself!" An **S** may ask, "Tell me again, how do you want it?" And an **I** may say, "I'm bored, how about doing it this way?"

After I present the first segment of my personality seminar, I ask participants how well they think they know their spouse, children, friends, peers and associates. Why would this be important? Simple: If your goal is making a difference by influencing people, you must have the right information. You need to understand others' needs, wants and preferences in order to better cater to their individual styles.

If you discover who people are (the *what, how* and *why* of their behaviors), you are way ahead of the game. You know an important part of their "people puzzle" that has been missing. You can look at their behaviors and know what to do and how to treat them. For instance, when you're working with a **C**, your mind will signal you: "Offer proof! Don't just *tell* them! Provide the data that verifies what you say!"

Classroom Communication

A teacher who doesn't understand these behavioral style issues may be frustrated too easily and tell **D** and **I** students, "Hey, you need to get yourself under control. Raise your hand, at least, before you try to take over my class!" Or, "Can't you just be quiet? Stay in your seat. You're talking too much. Listen instead of talk. Better yet, don't talk at all!"

A teacher who doesn't understand **S** and **C** types has little chance of connecting with students at the other extreme. No matter what, certain students just aren't going to participate heavily or initiate discussions. If they know more facts and details, their interjections in class sometimes impress, but often intimidate or irritate, their classmates.

These are all distinct personality types and they respond best to distinct approaches and techniques. By bringing them under our influence, instead of under our thumb (control), we can accomplish so much more.

Years ago, Dr. James Dobson spoke about student discipline at a teachers' convention. His bestselling book, *Dare to Discipline*, was brand-new and he was asked to share classroom insights. Afterward, a teacher approached him to say how much she enjoyed her job but wished she didn't have to be angry all the time to keep order in her classroom. Their conversation revealed how she allowed herself to be pushed until chaos reigned in her room, at which point she would climb up on her desk, blow a whistle and scream for control. Dr. Dobson explained that kids respond to *action*, not to *anger*, and the disruptions in her class would become more manageable if she took *action* before she became *angry*. She needed to draw her *action* line before she reached her *anger* line.

Can't you just see her **D** and **I** students getting restless and bored, then pushing her over the edge just to see her entertaining antics? Once they got her to do her "trick," they rewarded her with suitable behavior...until they got bored again. Can't you just feel the dismay and distress of her **S** and **C** students wondering how to cope with all this turmoil? Understanding *how* people behave would have made the classroom experience more enjoyable for this teacher and her students. She had been relying on *Controller* tactics while she could have been much more effective using *Influencer* techniques.

I want to treat my students as the individuals they are. I want them to honor each other in the same way. After completing a teachers' in-service training session, I received a comment that makes my point. A teacher wrote, "This really makes me aware of how different my students are and how they need to be treated differently. I have always tried to treat everyone the same or else I would be unfair. I realize now how unfair that was to these individuals."

This teacher learned that each person has special needs — that she could motivate, influence and inspire others through approaches that speak directly to them. In the classroom, I discovered that nothing is so unfair as trying to treat students the same and squeeze them all into the same mold. If we are going to communicate with others, it's important that we understand them. It's hard to have a solid relationship with someone you don't or can't comprehend!

D students (and adults) want your communication to be

targeted and to the point. "Business is business and play is business, and it's all a contest I want to win." They need choices, challenge and control over their situations. So I try to find something for **D** students to be in charge of while in my class. It doesn't seem to matter if it's a study group or handing out information, as long as they can direct it. (When they learn how much more powerful and effective *Influence* can be, some learn to deemphasize their *Controlling* tendencies.) Because it is their nature to challenge, test and push the limits, you will find success by learning how to work and communicate with them in ways that utilize their strengths and minimize their excesses.

In comparison, **I** students (and adults) are spontaneous, creative and animated. They seldom have a hidden agenda because they "talk" while others "think." An authority figure (teacher or supervisor) who is trying to get a project done may see them as an interruption, while they seem themselves as an inspiration. They have difficulty just sitting and listening. Because it's their nature to seek acceptance and approval, put them in the spotlight from time to time and provide the recognition they need. They love fun and interaction. Keep them on target with short-term goals. Break bigger tasks into small steps with accountability. They tend to start projects enthusiastically but underestimate the work involved, so make sure they have help completing their tasks. Again, learn how to enlist their cooperation, minimize their excesses and utilize their strengths, and you'll succeed.

S students (and adults) usually sit quietly and participate reluctantly when called on. They are people-conscious and want to make others feel included. In the classroom, I have tried to create a fun atmosphere with specific, familiar routines for them. **S** types need peace and harmony. They establish their own comfort zones and resist change. They can be hesitant starters because they want to clarify instructions, but they are usually great finishers. They strongly desire closure and complete projects that others neglect. They have difficulty saying no because they are naturally conflict-avoiders and people-pleasers. They don't want to be decision-makers, but they can be good "fulfillers" because they are sensitive to others and want to meet expectations. Learning to minimize their excesses and utilize their strengths creates a win-win situation for everyone.

C students (and adults) tend to work quietly and display confidence when answering questions. They know what they know and usually don't speculate about what they don't know. Accountability equals credibility, and they want to learn from people who are authorities, not novices. Quality answers and value determine what they buy into. In my classroom, they know I'm not the expert at everything. They see through people who pretend to be, and may even work to expose their errors. They want to comply with sensible rules and they expect fairness. They want to be respected for their knowledge and accuracy, and they expect similar performance from you. Set high standards and stick to them. By knowing how to work and communicate with them, you will achieve mutual success.

Talking Personality "Language"

In the classroom, teachers must always ask themselves, "How can I get young people to listen?" *Telling* is not *teaching,* and whether you're a teacher, parent, manager or worker, you want to be heard and understood. It's not enough to *tell;* we must *sell* our information. Here is an example showing why a one-size-fits-all teaching approach is inadequate:

In a TV documentary about teens and alcohol, some kids actually said, "Everybody does drugs and drinks alcohol." They were carefree and oblivious to any facts except that they were young and life is a party. "Do your parents know that you drink?" one teen was asked. "No, but we do, almost every weekend."

In one scene, some teenagers and one young adult of legal age were taken to a research building and shown some before-and-after effects of alcohol on the brain. It was literally warped. Typical grooves and ridges had become humps, lumps and deformations. The narrator said a 30-year-old brain subjected to alcohol could look like an 80-year-old brain, without the wisdom!

I thought about how such a "documentary" approach impacts attitudes among the four personality types. In my experience, this approach isn't as effective with *fast-paced* **D**s and **I**s. *Faster-paced* people tend not to *understand* something until they *experience* it, while *slower-paced* people tend to avoid *experiencing* things until they *understand* them. If you're wondering why this would fail to impact a **D** or an **I**, chances are that you're not either one!

An **I**-type student, looking at a computer printout of before-and-after effects of alcohol on the brain would not feel the impact of this data that an **S** or **C** student would. **I**s would be more inclined to think, "How would this affect how my friends see me? Can they even see my brain? Can I still have fun?" Use data alone and you'll lose the **I**s!

As a younger, invincible **D**, I would have thought, "So what? I can do more with half a brain than they could with a full brain anyway! I'm Superman — I can handle it!"

My wife has strong **S** and **C**, and the effect on her was just the opposite. She was astonished. "Honey, did you see that?

It's the most powerful thing I've ever seen in my whole life! That's why I don't drink! See what it does to your brain?" A **C** also thinks, "Research shows that alcohol can affect my decision or reasoning skills, so it's probably not good."

Fortunately for **D** and **I** students, the video used additional approaches. For **I**s, they showed what the outcome of this "good time" could be. They took teens to a junkyard and presented a car that had been wrecked. They asked viewers to imagine it was their car and they had been victims of the accident. They showed the hospital where all the passengers had died. Only the driver survived.

Then video clips showed anguished parents being notified by police. We followed them to the cemetery and listened as they spoke parting words to their children at the grave sites. An emotional appeal gets to **I**s.

For **D**s, the reality of prison and the consequences of their bad decisions and criminal actions were included. This brutal outcome might be the only effective method, demonstrating powerlessness to those who always want to be in control.

Using these concepts, how would you speak effectively to students about sexually-transmitted diseases? Provide facts and statistics about damage to the body and mind to **C**s. Show real physical effects with pictures. Seeing the risk to their secure future will help **S**s get the message. If risky behavior could damage their appearance and appeal to others, this could speak to them and to **I**s. Since **D**s tend to underestimate personal risk, they may be willing to challenge the odds, so they need defined limits that are watched carefully. Every circumstance presents a challenge to them, even sex.

When it comes to sex, **I** types are a special category — their "love language" tends to be *touch* and *words*. Whenever

I ask **I** teens why they are having sex, I know I will hear some variation of "I just want to feel loved." **I**s want recognition, acceptance and approval. As a parent, you can help meet that need. If you aren't providing a sense of belonging and nurturing (with accountability) to your **I** children, they will get it where they can.

An especially volatile situation exists when a **D** boy sees an **S** girl as a sexual conquest and she feels guilty when she says no. Peer pressure has amazing power among teens. Group dates, which provided safer social activities when parents were younger may now create pressure to "go along." It makes sense to know the dynamics among those in your teen's peer group. Help them create limits and healthy outlets for their emotions and energies. There's no claim that understanding **DISC** will give all teens the moral strength to say no to sex, drugs, alcohol, gangs or any other potential trainwrecks of youth, but it's a helpful weapon in their survival arsenal. (Speaking of gangs, I've heard that parents of **D** children never need worry that their child will *join* a gang — they are much more likely to *start* one of their own!)

Attention And Recognition

A parent asked once if I think there is a difference in *attention* and *recognition* — "A lot of children are just trying to get attention," she added. I explained that for many **I**s, there is little difference. If they can have fun, draw attention to themselves, and get recognized because of it, all the better! The three often go hand-in-hand.

However, more reserved personality types don't want their actions to draw attention. **C**s may want to be recognized for the quality of their work and **S**s for their service, but they aren't looking for increased notoriety.

Let's say you want to thank each type for some favor they did for you. Dr. Robert Rohm says each type will predictably handle your thanks in a different way:

- A **D** may think, "You're right — who else could have helped you as much or as well? You *should* recognize that!"
- An **I** may think, "So do I get a party? A plaque? A small gold statuette? My name in the paper? Who else have you told?"
- An **S** may think, "Oh, please don't make a fuss in front of everyone. Maybe a little memento, or cash, and a sincere note."
- A **C** may think, "Hmmmm, what do you want now?"

"What about *attention* and *love?*" the same parent asked me. Paying attention and showing love are not necessarily the same. You can be sitting in a room with your child and never hold them, touch them, or tell them you love them, but still be paying attention to them. Beyond attention, children want to be told and shown that parents love them.

Understanding some of these key differences in personality styles and knowing that they are seeking *different* answers for the *same* questions, we must present, explain, and talk to each of the styles differently. For instance, let's look at self-image.

Personalities And Self-Image

Among the faster-paced, outgoing styles, a **D**'s self-image is naturally pretty good. They believe in themselves even when no one else will. An **I**'s self-image is a reflection they "catch" from other people as they make them happy or cause them to laugh, and as they are the stars of the show.

When we look at the slower-paced, more reserved types, an **S**'s self-image is based in their need to serve and help others, coupled with their perception of life as smooth, with a dependable, steady routine. And a **C**'s self-image is strongly tied to their ability to make right decisions and take actions that validate their high standards and expectations.

Do You Vent Or Stuff Your Feelings?

S and **C** types tend to stuff their emotional responses, unlike **D** and **I** types, who vent and vocalize their emotions. I mentioned earlier that Wendy would rather not say something than have her words hurt someone's feelings. Instead of revealing their feelings, reserved people often hold them inside. **S** types may not want to be a bother, and **C** types may not want to admit a need for help. **C**s, especially, run into this problem when what they're doing isn't working — remember their need to be correct? Very rarely will they volunteer an uninvited opinion or guess if they don't know an answer.

When most **C**s speak, they are not flamboyant; they consider every word as important. So when they speak, listen — they do their research. Contrast this to an **I**, whose "life" is talking. You can be assured that their important words are surrounded by lots of filler. It's almost like **C**s talk when necessary, and **I**s talk out of necessity!

Do you remember Thoreau's line about people leading "lives of quiet desperation?" If that describes **S**s and **C**s, we **D**s and **I**s don't understand it. Nor do we "go quietly into the good night"!

We Think Differently

Can it really be this simple — that different personality types think differently, even *predictably,* in almost all areas of their lives? Is it possible that there are understandable patterns that function as lenses through which we look at the same things but see differently?

At the seminar I mentioned earlier, Ken Voges asked me, "You do know that you think differently from her, right?" (He was referring to the *slower-paced,* more reserved lady sitting next to me.) I replied, "Of course I think differently from her." *Wait a minute!* I *do* think differently from her! And I think differently from my mom, my dad, two of my sisters *and* my wife — all of whom are **S**s and **C**s. But I think a lot like my other sister, who is an **I**!

I was on to something! My **C** father sat right next to that **S** lady in the seminar, so I asked him, "What do you think about what Ken was saying, that we really do think differently?" Predictably, he replied, "Let me think about it."

Hmmmm. We were in the same seminar and both of us saw what happened. Yet my father had to think about what he was going to tell me. I had expected him to do something against his nature by giving me an immediate response!

This means your children don't think and act as you do, either. You have your personality style and they have theirs. Even if you share a basic **D**, **I**, **S** or **C** perspective, your individual blend of these four types creates a style that is different from others you live and work with.

How do you cater to these differences? How do you teach or parent to them? We can learn and then apply what we know. For instance:

- Since **D**s need challenge, choice and control, we can set up environments that include these parameters.
- Since **I**s need recognition, acceptance and approval, we can engineer environments to include those.
- Since **S**s need appreciation, safety and security, we can create environments that honor, even celebrate, them.

- Since a **C**'s needs include quality, data and value, we can set up environments that recognize those needs.

Understanding these differences also means that we can see underlying factors in people's behaviors — we can filter our perceptions and see beyond the obvious. A mother at one of my parenting seminars gave an example of testing the differences in her children. Just for fun, she messed up her hair just before her family left for church. She wondered if her prediction of their reactions would be correct.

Her youngest, an **I**, exclaimed, "Ooh — yuck, Mom!" Her **S** middle child said, "Hey, don't say that! You'll hurt Mom's feelings." Her oldest, a **C** child, agreed, "Well, I don't want to hurt her feelings, either, but she sure needs to know the truth." (Chances are that a **D** child would not have delivered much background information but would have spoken in bullet points: "You've got a hair problem — comb it!")

Rather than feeling offended, she felt vindicated — she knew her children well and didn't doubt their love in the slightest. She had learned and could translate each child's language.

Chapter 5:
CAMPFIRES
AND BONFIRES

"Reality TV" shows are popular at the time I'm working on this book. They often feature people who haven't got a clue, trying to figure out how to win and get what they want. Eventually, they adapt and succeed or they leave in defeat. Either way, when the TV show is over, they have to return to *The Real World* — for real!

Have you noticed that, no matter which series you watch, there are people whom:
- You like
- Kind of like
- Love
- Love to hate
- Just don't like at all?

Some of these characters are totally out of touch in the ways they act and treat others, even in how they treat themselves. They don't understand how they come across, and their own experiences, beliefs, opinions and personalities form their version of reality. Facts that are obvious to everyone else disappear when run through their filters!

In my classes, how we are viewed and judged by others is called *People Perception*. How do you think others see you? And just as important, how do you see yourself? We're going to look at some of the strengths and struggles of your personality in this chapter, beginning with a look at your "campfire."

What does a campfire provide for you? Here is a short list:
- Supplies warmth
- Gives light
- Offers aroma
- Affords safety and security

In other words, it meets some basic needs. You can also cook on your campfire and scare away wild animals!

Thinking about campfires, are there some areas in your life where you are (*this is going to sound strange*) "camping out?" I mean, you feel very comfortable around certain ideas, attitudes, outlooks, beliefs and behaviors, so you stay close and don't stray from the comfort of your little campsite.

Even irritability, impatience, jealousy, dishonesty and other negative attitudes may be providing a sense of warmth and comfort. Otherwise, people wouldn't be doing them! If someone is constantly arguing and yelling, maybe that's what they want to do. It may be a personality trait, that we always want control (**D**), or always want acceptance (**I**), or always want to avoid conflict (**S**), or always want to be right (**C**).

Think about this: People who are possessive and untrusting are trying to get what they want, and through their negative behaviors, they may be able to keep another person close to them for a while. The drawback is that their behavior, which seems beneficial in the beginning, ultimately destroys relationships. In other words, what first attracts people to the campfire may eventually drive them away.

This isn't just my humble-but-accurate opinion. At Miami University, psychologist James C. Coyne asked 45 female college students to talk on the phone for 20 minutes with other women, some of whom were depressed. Although the students weren't told about the depression, they indicated much less interest in spending time with the those women than with those who were not depressed. It's a common cycle: Unhappy people often drive away people whose support they need, worsening their depression and intensifying their need for support.

When we realize that people are backing away from our campfires, we should ask why. Perhaps our fire, which seems warming to us, is too hot for them! If it's burning them and they can't find *insulation,* they will create *isolation* — away from you and all your negative attitudes and offensive behaviors!

So let's think about developing new attitudes and beliefs regarding campfires and comfort zones, keeping this in mind:

**It's not so much where you're *leaving from,*
but where you're *going to,* that counts!**

Personal growth means leaving a comfortable fire, where you have felt safe and warm, and moving toward a different place that isn't comfortable...yet! It's normal to ask ourselves why we would ever choose to head in a new direction. Great question! The answer is that growth is a *process,* and the first step in the direction of growth is *willingness to change.*

Do you get this picture? You're at "Campfire A" (*see the next page*), where you've always felt comfortable. But no one else has gathered around the campfire with you, and people who stop by don't stay very long! Something's wrong with what you're doing, but you're getting some satisfaction from it or you wouldn't be doing it. Now, for your personal growth and increased satisfaction, I'm asking you to move out of your comfort zone and head into the darkness — and I'm telling you now that the darkness is only temporary. Of course, walking into dark-

The CONTROLLER'S BONFIRE drives people away

- Impatient
- Jealous
- Bossy
- Possessive
- Critical
- Manipulative

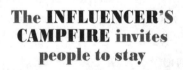

LEAVE YOUR COMFORT ZONE

- Patient
- Trusting
- Considerate
- Sharing
- Affirming
- Truthful

The INFLUENCER'S CAMPFIRE invites people to stay

ness won't seem like the right thing to do much of the time. Whether you're 5, 15 or 55, it's going to be a little scary! I'm asking you to find another light at a more appropriate campfire. And believe me, many of the people who left your campfire when it got too hot will be waiting there for you.

The Fire Within

In the classroom, we talk about fire as an attractor. On a camping trip, an inviting campfire becomes the focal point. People are drawn to it for warmth, safety, food, friendship. (Can't you almost hear the musical strains of *Koombyah?*) But it's really important to keep the campfire where it belongs. If unrestrained and improperly used, something meant to bring comfort can bring calamity.

It's the same for the strengths of our personality styles. When we balance our style's natural gifts and talents, we create an inviting and secure atmosphere for others. Without restraint, your fire can threaten people and destroy what has been built up around it. This concept doesn't require a lot of explanation — can you think of some examples in your own life where this may be true?

The following four pages provide practical application for our styles and relationships. On one side of the line, the fire is raging and the result is too much heat and too many sparks. Others feel threatened, exposed and unsafe, but since it is your fire, you may not be aware. It's also possible that your style isn't blazing out of control at all — but really, *other people's perceptions are everything!* You may still be comfortable, even while they are backing away.

When do you run the greatest risk of becoming a raging bonfire instead of a warming campfire? When you are tired or stressed or unaware of others' needs, you're less likely to "tend the fire" and more likely to "fan the flames."

Your "campfire" strengths are listed on the right side — not just positive *traits* but *how we see ourselves and our motivations.* The left side list is "bonfire" struggles, negative traits that arise when our positive traits become extreme or undisciplined.

It's often hard for us to recognize when we have drifted into "bonfire" behavior, partly because it still feels comfortable (or at least normal) to us. A good clue might be to notice how few people are feeling warmed and comforted around our fire. As noted before, the people you don't see are waiting for you to leave your "bonfire" and return to your welcoming "campfire!"

If you're at all like me, you will probably like reading your own "campfire" list but not your "bonfire" list. Some of my students feel insulted when they read it. *"Mr. H, that's not me at all!"* We can argue all day that people misunderstand our attitudes and behaviors — and we can even be right — but what people think about us if often more potent than the truth. It can be humbling to learn how others sometimes see us.

"D" BONFIRE
(how others may see us)

"D" CAMPFIRE
(how we may see ourselves)

Arrogant	Bold
Combative	Competitive
Reckless	Risk-Taking
Headstrong	Determined
Autonomous	Independent
Tactless	Outspoken
Dictatorial	Decisive
Pushy	Assertive
Predatory	Pioneering
Offensive	Confronting
Ruthless	Strategic
Rude	Direct
Disrespectful	Self-Confident
Conceited	Self-Assured
Intimidating	Challenging
Dogmatic	Authoritative
Defiant	Daring
Impatient	Ambitious
Demanding	Persistent
Obsessive	Goal-Oriented

"I" BONFIRE
(how others may see us)

"I" CAMPFIRE
(how we may see ourselves)

"I" BONFIRE	"I" CAMPFIRE
Indiscriminate	Trusting
Unrealistic	Optimistic
Manipulative	Charming
Frivolous	Amusing
Fickle	Sociable
Exaggerating	Convincing
Impulsive	Spontaneous
Gushy	Enthusiastic
Situational	Relational
Gossipy	Communicative
Shallow	Lighthearted
Unfocused	Flexible
Effusive	Articulate
Illogical	Passionate
Self-Promoting	Talkative
Distractible	Imaginative
Frenetic	Energetic
Loud	Gregarious
Fast-Talking	Persuasive
Impractical	Ingenious

"S" BONFIRE
(how others may see us)

"S" CAMPFIRE
(how we may see ourselves)

"S" BONFIRE	"S" CAMPFIRE
Complacent	Even-Tempered
Unemotional	Stable
Patsy	Helpful
Dispassionate	Steady
Hesitant	Satisfied
Timid	Peaceful
Dependent	Team-Oriented
Spineless	Cooperative
Closemouthed	Good Listener
Slow	Methodical
Passive	Patient
Monotonous	Predictable
Enabling	Supportive
Self-Inflicting	Empathetic
Possessive	Loyal
Dishonest	Nonconfronting
Fragile	Sensitive
Resistant	Traditional
Uninvolved	Neutral
Grudging	Forgiving

"C" BONFIRE
(how others may see us)

"C" CAMPFIRE
(how we may see ourselves)

Severe	Modest
Picky	Precise
Scheming	Calculating
Nosy	Observant
Unsociable	Solitary
Distrustful	Cautious
Fixated	Detailed
Perfectionist	Exacting
Faultfinding	Accurate
Rigid	Compliant
Uncaring	Efficient
Compulsive	Orderly
Emotionless	Logical
Fretful	Conscientious
Stubborn	Consistent
Theoretical	Idealistic
Suspicious	Analytical
Prying	Questioning
Evasive	Private
Superior	Excellent

This event opened my eyes wide: Wendy and I were walking through a shopping mall when a former student spotted me and said, "Hey, Mr. Hinojosa! How's it going? I just wanted to tell you I really enjoyed your class, and thanks for helping me set my goals."

My high **I** style always welcomes this kind of recognition, especially in front of others. Wendy gave me a puzzled glance and we continued walking. A few minutes later, another former student, now in college, exclaimed, "Hey, Mr. Hinojosa! Thanks for inspiring me to go for my dreams. I'm working on a degree in science." I was on fire — recognition is *goooood!*

Wendy was wearing that perplexed expression again. I asked, *"What?"* and she replied, "Who *are* you? All of these students are coming up and talking to you. You're so excited and in such a good mood."

Whatever "high" I was experiencing was about to crash well below sea-level. Why was Wendy so confused and upset with me? She added, "You seem to genuinely have a great rapport with these students...." (here comes the "but") *"but why* don't you act like this with your own daughter?"

I stood in the middle of the mall, stunned. I realized I was two different people, depending on where I was. "Campfire Pete" showed up at school: fun, encouraging, outgoing and patient. But "Bonfire Pete" came home moody, brooding, impatient, demanding and not very encouraging. At that moment, I was faced with another opportunity to grow. Was I really an *Influencer* at school and a *Controller* at home? Knowing better isn't always doing better. I thought of the words of Sir Winston Churchill:

Men occasionally stumble over the truth, but then pick themselves up and hurry off as if nothing happened.

How would I respond to this encounter with truth? Was it possible that I spent more time encouraging other peoples' children than my own? Students came to me for help, but my own children barely knew me. I needed to grow and change.

I tell my students the following story to make the point that change isn't optional when someone points out the need, even if you're not aware of it:

Imagine that you're about to buy the most stylish jeans. You put them on and look in the three-way mirror — all three ways! You've got *The Look!* But you're so excited about the jeans that you don't realize you've forgotten to zip up. To show off your new source of self-esteem, you decide to wear the jeans around the mall. The sales clerk takes one look at you and gives you an up-and-down gesture with her thumb. Unfortunately, you see it as "thumbs up," not "zip up."

Wherever you walk, people stare at you. They try to get your attention, and you're thinking, "Man, this is awesome! These jeans were worth the money — people can't keep their eyes off me!" Finally, a mall security guard walks up to you: "Hey, your pants...."

You can't believe it. "Wow! Even people who work here want to know where I got *The Look!*"

"Hey, you need to zip it up!" *Whhhaat?* You look down and your bubble bursts! What do you do next? You don't say, "*Well, duhhh... I meant to do that!*" You fix it quickly and hope you're not going to be prime-time news with all of your friends.

However, when we see or hear the truth about our *character*, many of us reject it. We keep moving ahead as if nothing had happened. I heard about a man who was driving home from work when his cell phone rang. It was his wife, warning him urgently: "I just heard on the news that there's a car going the wrong way on the freeway. Please be careful!" He replied, "I'm there right now, and it's not just *one* car — it's *hundreds* of them!"

Are there areas in your life where people have said you're driving against the flow, or your zipper is down, but you didn't get it, or you pretended it was just what you intended?

If you have a lot of **D** in your personality style, it might work like this: When someone tells you that you come across as a little pushy or bossy, you are offended. "Who are they to tell me that? They don't know me!" So you find three of your "lower **D**" friends, whom you can easily order around, and "ask" them forcefully, "I'm not pushy, am I? Tell me I'm not bossy! *Tell me!*"

They respond as you hope: "*Oh nooooo*, you're not pushy or bossy at all." And you breathe a huge sigh of relief. For a second, you thought you were going to have to change!

It's not just **D**s who need a change. We all have areas where we need to see things as they truly are and not just as our personality style's "filter" interprets them.

Artist Ingrid Walter said, "Whenever I am sketching a portrait, I use a little trick to reveal errors in perspective. I occasionally hold the picture in front of a mirror. Its reflection reveals all my mistakes: an eye too high, a chin too bold, a mouth askew. When it's obvious by this reflection what I need to do to make my piece better, I can easily change it before it is finished."

You get the point, don't you? We need another perspective if we are going to see ourselves and our behaviors more realistically. Ms. Walter said, "If we stand back for a moment and *reflect on our own behavior* and *make the necessary minor changes,* we can transform it into a work of art."

Author Ken Blanchard says, "Feedback is the breakfast of champions." One of my students said it's like we have a certain picture in our minds about ourselves, and when someone tries to alter that image, we do everything we can to avoid the process. What if, the next time someone tries to change your picture of yourself, you respond with an open, teachable attitude? I'm not suggesting that you become a target for abuse or constant criticism; just think about stumbling over the truth.

If your *Influencer Incorporated* company is going to increase in profit and productivity, you must understand the perception of your "customers." Many companies use a "suggestion box" effectively. They say, "Let us know how we can serve you. Tell us what we're doing right, and tell us how can serve you better." If a company really wants to improve, it doesn't see comments as an attack but as a source for improvement.

During the Great Depression, a boy stopped at a drug store and asked if he could use the telephone to call a doctor. The pharmacist gave permission and overheard one side of the conversation:

"Doctor, do you need to hire a boy to run errands for you? Oh, you already pay a boy to do that? Well, are you satisfied with his work, or are you lookin' for another boy? He's doin' a good job, huh? Okay, thanks anyway." The boy hung up the phone and was walking out of the store when the druggist interrupted. "Young fella, if that doctor ain't looking for an errand boy, we are. You can work for me!" And the boy replied, "Thanks, but I've already got a job. I'm the Doc's errand boy. I was just checkin' up on myself to see how I'm doin'!"

How can you know when you need to change the picture? This is where you plug in what you know about your "company" and your personality style.

Check up on yourself! Use your "Assets and Liabilities" list (Chapter 8), your "Strengths and Struggles" (Chapters 5 and 6), your "Brand Name" description (Chapters 1 and 8), and other insights you develop from this book as a standard for comparison when others make comments about your character or behavior.

Study, too, the differences between your out-of-control behaviors and your under-control behaviors. Out of control, there is a good chance you're in *Controller* mode and the last to recognize it! Read over your personality "Strengths and Struggles" list periodically, and ask yourself honestly, "Am I acting like a *Controller* or am I being an *Influencer*? Am I coming across in ways that build effective, long-term relationships?"

This aspect of the personality information has helped me not to become offended or resistant to changing my own picture. None of us wants to have poor relationships, but many have never had an objective standard by which to see when we are out of control.

Having both a standard to live by and knowing your personality traits — when you are in *Controller* mode and in *Influencer* mode — will enable you to adapt better and become more effective. The alternative is to continue stumbling over the truth and hurrying off as if nothing has happened.

Chapter 6:
FOLLOW THE SIGNS

If you're a visual learner, you will probably appreciate these pictures, illustrating the four basic personality types. Four colors and four highway signs identify them, and you'll see a correlation between the colors, the signs and the behaviors of each type.

Ken Voges introduced me to color associations for each of the four DISC types, based on *The Wagner Color Response Report.* (Ken, by the way, is a Houston-based consultant and coauthor of *Understanding How Others Misunderstand You,* with Dr. Ron Braund.) The connection between the colors and the highway signs occurred to me shortly afterward.

For many students in my classes and attendees at business seminars, this combination of colors and road signs has been an easy way to remember characteristic traits of each basic type.

Check out the explanatory chart on the next page.

Color: **RED** — Tends to create an environment filled with energy and action. People who stare at red experience an increase in both blood pressure and pulse rate. With red as a background, objects tend to appear bigger and bolder. Red highway signs announce orders that we must obey, including STOP, YIELD, DO NOT ENTER and WRONG WAY! They tend to be "bullet commands" rather than informational, and they require immediate action. They answer the question, *"What to do?"*

Color: **GREEN** — Tends to cause a favorable body response and is easiest on the eye. Green-colored backgrounds make people feel secure and cared for. Green highway signs provide directions: how many miles before you get where you want to go, what part of a road you are on, and where to find information about places you want to go. They tell us in whose honor a bridge or highway has been named. Green is also used for the words on white signs about parking regulations. They answer the question, *"Where to go?"*

Color: **BLUE** — Tends to communicate harmony and peace. Research shows that light blue is most effective in calming the mind. Blue signs tell about motorist services and provide guidance: where safety rest areas and phones are, where to exit for food or sleep, where hospitals and police services are, where a litter barrel is so you won't throw your trash on the highway, who has adopted a section of highway to keep clean, and where to carpool with other drivers. They answer the question, *"How to get there?"*

Color: **YELLOW** — Tends to communicate caution and warns of danger when associated with black letters or symbols. Yellow is the first color the adult human eye notices. Over extended periods, it can create feelings of anxiety. Yellow signs tell where school zones are and where children may be playing. They warn about railroad crossings and traffic lights, dead ends and roads with no outlets, a bridge ahead with ice, and when a lane is ending. *They answer the questions "What to bring?" and "Why are we going?"*

The Buffet Of Life

If you could see life as a buffet line at an all-you-can-eat restaurant, you'd see me gobbling from the **D** buffet every day. I'm mixing metaphors here, but **D** is a mainstay of my diet — and I choose **I** for dessert! Because of my personality style's preferences, I like the way **D** tastes in my mouth. Challenge, Control and Choice are very satisfying to me, even though others may find that **D** leaves a bad taste in their mouths.

Since my **I** traits are very strong, I also love the taste of Recognition, Popularity and Attention! At life's buffet, you would see me eating from both of these tables while turning up my nose at what **S** and **C** types find delicious. Of course, **D** and **I** intake alone won't create a balanced diet, but it's what I like!

Each person has a preferred "diet," and left to their own devices, that's what they would always choose to fill up on, even though they're allowed to eat all they want from all four buffet tables. My style has its own "minimum daily requirements" and if I don't get enough, I feel hungry — even weak — so I thrive on them.

It's not just that my own style's basic **D** and **I** needs drive my activities and shape my viewpoint, but my greatest fears involve not having them met. How do I feel when my appetites aren't satisfied? I feel:
- Out of control
- Frustrated
- Anxious
- Worried
- Angry

And I want to get back in control immediately!

My instinctive response is to use all the **D** and **I** tricks and techniques I can think of to meet my needs, reestablish my position and maintain my comfort. The same is true for **S** and **C** types, too, but their tricks and techniques differ. We all tend to do what we can to get what we need.

When I was a teenager, I would do just about anything to meet my needs for acceptance, popularity and recognition. So I did good things, but I also made my share of poor choices. Until I learned that I was in control of my behaviors, I always did what came naturally, and there are times I still slip up. My goal now is to be appropriate in the way I behave, so there are times when I rein in my natural tendencies and do what is less comfortable for me, so I can work better with others.

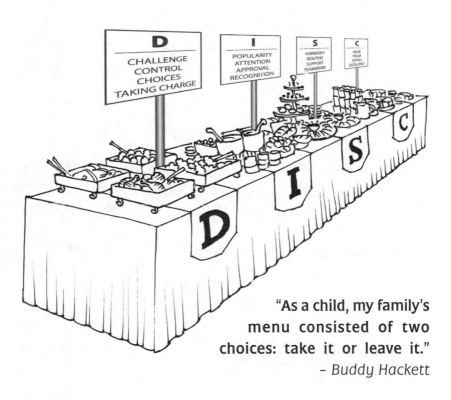

"As a child, my family's menu consisted of two choices: take it or leave it."
– *Buddy Hackett*

What are some of the "favorite foods" of each type?
Ds eat deliberately from the buffet of:

- Challenge
- Control
- Choices
- Taking charge

Is eat impulsively from the buffet of:

- Popularity
- Attention
- Approval
- Recognition

Ss eat slowly from the buffet of:

- Harmony
- Routine
- Support
- Teamwork

Cs eat cautiously from the buffet of:

- Value (don't waste my time, money, effort)
- Proof
- Details
- Excellence (if not perfection)

Since "**DISC**overing" this information, I've been learning how to take in limited amounts of **S** and **C** nourishment, too. These may not be my natural favorites but, as I develop tastebuds that can appreciate the differences, I am able to add flavor and variety to my life.

You can, too! Learn to appreciate how people with other personality styles fill in your blind spots, and work at developing habits that other types do naturally. Include opposite styles on your team to help you become more aware. Life is more than a buffet — it's a banquet!

DISC With An Accent!

As a high school student, I studied Spanish. Even though I have Hispanic roots and took two years of Spanish classes, I never became fluent. It was especially uncomfortable speaking the language around people for whom it was their native tongue. They would ask, "Habla Espanol?" and I would mumble, "Un poquito...."

It was obvious just how *poquito* when they spoke in full sentences and I understood only two or three words! I felt so uncomfortable that, most of the time, I just gave up and admitted that I couldn't understand. When I spoke more than a few words, my American accent was obvious. I've tried faking my way through it, but the fact is that I just don't speak Spanish well.

I speak English because it's how I grew up, and it's what I'm comfortable speaking. If I moved to a Spanish-speaking country, I would have no option — speaking the local language would become necessary.

You have a "personality language" that you feel most comfortable speaking. For instance, my personality style grew up speaking **D** and **I**. If your basic language is **S**, then my **D** language is foreign to you. Huge misunderstandings are likely when we try to communicate. A key for interpersonal success is learning the **D**, **I**, **S** or **C** language that is least familiar to you. (**D** and **S** are opposites, as are **I** and **C**.) This is easier said than done, but don't stop! Learning a new language is uncomfortable, but in the end, it will be worth it. Keep working to become fluent in all four personality languages.

- **D**s tends to speak more forcefully and authoritatively than the other types. Expect that they will speak to you with direct, bottom-line and to-the-point words, so do the same! My accent sounds like Challenge, Control and Competition. When someone speaks to me in the **D** language, I understand.

- **I**s rely on humor and emotional appeals to get their points across. They use lots of hand gestures and facial expressions. Conversation will cover wide areas and be spontaneous. Flow with them! I speak **I** fluently, with its accent on Recognition, Popularity and Attention, and I understand when someone speaks **I** to me.

I need help hearing and translating the languages spoken by **S**s and **C**s because they are different. In fact, I think some of their words don't even translate into my preferred languages!

- **S**s use peaceable words that calm tension and bring understanding. They choose their words so that they don't hurt anyone's feelings or come across in a negative way. Be sensitive and attentive — listen carefully! The **S** style's accent sounds like Steadiness, Predictability and Closure.

- **C**s speak with logic and objectivity, searching for meaning and details. They tend to speak when they have something insightful to add. They explain with details and facts. So do your homework and make sense! The accent of people who speak **C** sounds like Data, Accuracy and Logic.

How do we feel when we're unable to hear or speak our language? What happens? We feel out of control. Because of my strong **D** and the need to feel in control of every aspect of my life, this is not my "happy place." I feel frustrated, anxious, worried, angry. Other styles may have a slower fuse, but eventually, they reach this place, too. Being so strongly **D**, I'll take direct action to get control back. Other styles use less direct methods, but their goal is also not to be at the mercy of people who devalue them. The way I go about it, however, when I am not self-controlled, doesn't communicate well or build solid relationships.

Whatever our styles, we tend to "hear" others through our own language preferences. We evaluate *their* words using the filter of *our* personality language.

For instance, while **S**s don't like challenge and conflict at all, **D**s think of it almost as sport or recreation. So **S** types find it easy to hear more harshness in a **D**'s tone than may have been intended.

On the other hand, **S**s tend to keep their objections to themselves rather than stir things up. This may be interpreted incorrectly as agreement because **D**s are sure to speak up if they disagree and expect others to do so, as well.

It's not always what we *say* but how people *hear* us that matters. To communicate effectively with each style, there are "Dos and Don'ts" for each basic type. People interpret what we mean according to their own blends of **D**, **I**, **S** and **C**.

I've provided a list of suggestions on the following pages to explain each type's perspective. You can improve your two-way communication skills by keying in on these clues.

Just be aware that you are still speaking a "foreign language" when you adjust your style to work with someone else's. I must always be careful when speaking the **S** or **C** languages. I speak with a pretty thick **D-I** accent and may not be as fluent or clear as I think I am.

These charts show the preferences of each basic type.

Personality Perspective	D	I	S	C
Outlook	Like to Lead Be In Charge	Like to Persuade Others	Like to Support & Help	Like Consistent Quality & Excellence
Blind Spot	Feelings of Others	Recalling Past Commit-ments	Moving Quickly on Problems & Issues	Seeing the Big Picture & Feelings
Response Under Pressure	Abrasive & Tough	Careless & Unpredict-able	Hesistant & Indecisive	Picky & Pessimistic
Secret Fear	Being Taken Advantage Of	Loss of Social Recognition	Change & Confronta-tion	The Unknown or Undefined
When They Feel Cornered	Head-On Attack	Emotional Attack	Stubborn Defense	Technical Defense
Likes To Do Things This Way	The Fastest Way	The Fun Way	The Traditional Way	The Proper Way
Approach To Tasks	Do It Now	Make It Fun	Work Together	Do It Right
Approach To People	Let's See What You Can Do	Let's Have Fun	Let's Do Something Together	Let's Do Our Own Part

Personality Perspective	D	I	S	C
Want to Know	What Is There to Get Done?	Who Is Going to Be There?	How Can I Help or Support You?	Why Are We Doing This?
Want You to Be	Direct & To The Point	Excited & Optimistic	Sincere & Non-Confronting	Credible
Dream Of	Accomplish-ments & Money	Being a Star	Security for Family	Long-Term Profit
Process Information By Asking	What Will Work?	Is It Fun?	Give Me Time?	Is It Logical?
Driven By	My Will	My Feelings	My Trust	My Intellect
Key Strength	Firm	Fun	Friendly	Factual
Key Struggle	To Be Friendly	To Be Factual	To Be Firm	To Be Fun
Secret To Their Success	To Be Under Authority	To Slow Down & Focus	To Be More Decisive	To Be More Caring

Personality Perspective	D	I	S	C
Motivating Statement	You're the One in Charge!	You're The Greatest!	You're So Dependable!	You're a Good Thinker!
"Killer" Statement	You Don't Matter!	You Think That's Funny!	You Let Me Down!	You Made a Mistake!
How They Defend	Confront	Shift Blame	Withdraw	Be Logical
Basic Priority	Power	People	Pace	Procedure
Will Seek First To	Solve Problems	Persuade Others	Maintain Peace	Uphold Principles
Buying Method	Quickly – New	Impulsively – Feeling	Slowly – Traditional	Cautiously – Value
Personal Decor	Large Desk & Awards	Flashy, Trendy, Fun Pictures	Family Pictures, Personal	Unique & Functional
Organizational Method	Accessible, Practical, Not Neat	"Piles" System	Systematic & Traditional	Highly Organized

Personality Perspective	D	I	S	C
Body Language	Big Gestures, Leans Forward, Advancing	Expressive, Friendly Posture, Amusing	Gentle Gestures, Reassuring	Unemotional, Controlled Gestures, Assessing
Speech	Direct, Abrupt, Always Doing Something	Talkative, Distracted Easily	Conversational, Warm, Friendly Listener	Clarifying, Monotone, Emotionless
Energizing Recharge	Competition, Physical Activity	Interaction, Social Activity	Retreat, Indirect Activity	Solitude, Cognitive Activity
Best Goals	Challenging	Short -Term	Evenly Paced	Long -Term
Focus	Achieving the Goal	Getting the Prize	Teamwork	Doing It Right the First Time, Quality
Ideal Environment	Upbeat, Powerful	Friendly, Exciting	Stable, Harmonious	Structure, Quality Control
Percentage Of Population	15%	30%	35%	20%
Basic Needs	Challenge, Control & Choice	Recognition, Popularity	Harmony, Appreciation	Proof, Value

If this is your style, practice these Communication Dos and Don'ts

Note: These guidelines permit "authority figures" to operate in *Influence Mode* rather than *Control Mode*. Children provide a ready example, but these principles can be applied thoughtfully in virtually all relationships.

If the child is a

Provide your child with choices whenever possible.
Avoid arguing or threatening.
Allow some opportunities for personal control.
Set and enforce limits.
Avoid power plays and power struggles.

If the child is a

Find ways to have fun when working with your child.
Model firm resistance to peer pressure.
Provide clear, simple—even written—instructions.
Avoid withholding praise or acceptance as discipline.
Listen, and encourage development of verbal skills.

If the child is a

Be extra careful of hurtful words and tone of voice.
Encourage, but do not force, decision-making.
Avoid expecting or compelling individual competitiveness.
Reassure often, and schedule personal time.
Avoid unfavorable comparisons to others.

If the child is a

Provide time for deciding and adjusting to change.
Teach that perfection is not required for success.
Allow opportunities to discover their own mistakes.
Provide quality answers to their involved questions.
Recognize and praise practical problem-solving skills.

If this is your style, practice these Communication Dos and Don'ts

Note: These guidelines permit "authority figures" to operate in *Influence Mode* rather than *Control Mode*. Children provide a ready example, but these principles can be applied thoughtfully in virtually all relationships.

If the child is a (D)

> *Enforce predefined limits with predetermined discipline.*
> *Avoid backing away from challenges or confrontations.*
> *Be consistent, and avoid allowing for "wiggle room."*
> *Be brief and specific in giving guidance and correction.*
> *Guard your reserves; maintain control of the situation.*

If the child is a (I)

> *Recognize your tendency to be overly lenient.*
> *Teach consequences rather than rescuing your child.*
> *Listen as much as you talk—don't be overly distracted.*
> *Demonstrate how you control your own impulsiveness.*
> *Be specific in writing out assignments and to-do lists.*

If the child is a (S)

> *Slow your pace, while teaching them adaptability.*
> *Show sincere appreciation in your comments.*
> *Provide advance warning of upcoming changes.*
> *Correct and praise privately—praise more.*
> *Allow time for learning to make confident decisions.*

If the child is a 

> *Be specific, rather than general, in your praise.*
> *Control your own impulsiveness; expect caution.*
> *Choose your words carefully when making corrections.*
> *Listen carefully to the meaning behind comments.*
> *Provide for your child to have quiet time, alone.*

(Reprinted with permission from *Getting To Know You*, © 2002, Chris Carey (CreativeCommunication Publications)

If this is your style, practice these Communication Dos and Don'ts

Note: These guidelines permit "authority figures" to operate in *Influence Mode* rather than *Control Mode*. Children provide a ready example, but these principles can be applied thoughtfully in virtually all relationships.

If the child is a (D)

{
Allow some control without being controlled.
Recognize their desire for some independence.
Expect and prepare to meet challenge.
Be consistent and firm on matters of principle.
Win decisively, if you must win—without guilt.
}

If the child is an (I)

{
Don't enable irresponsibility by rescuing them.
Write down step-by-step instructions, in duplicate.
Instill organizational habits by repeated practice.
Recognize "smooth talk" and require details.
Be careful about giving permission without limits.
}

If the child is a (S)

{
Avoid sheltering them from healthy conflict.
Teach them how to vocalize hurts and attitudes.
Help them gain confidence in making decisions.
Find opportunities for their independent success.
Encourage them to read "people skill" books.
}

If the child is a (C)

{
Honor their need for privacy and dignity.
Understand their controlled, less emotional responses.
Find what is praiseworthy, but don't flatter them.
Provide time for recharging without interruption.
Demonstrate self-acceptance and tolerance.
}

If this is your style, practice these Communication Dos and Don'ts

Note: These guidelines permit "authority figures" to operate in *Influence Mode* rather than *Control Mode*. Children provide a ready example, but these principles can be applied thoughtfully in virtually all relationships.

If the child is a

Avoid "improving" their projects or accomplishments.
Help them understand wise limits in taking risks.
Understand their need to "go and do."
Establish reasonable, achievable standards.
Praise their ability to set and reach goals.

If the child is a

Avoid bogging down in details they won't understand.
Commend accomplishments and strengths often.
Approve of improvement; don't expect perfection.
Make time for laughter, activity, fun and spontaneity.
Listen to their stories without dismissing them.

If the child is a

Learn to articulate your feelings more warmly.
Provide detailed explanations for tasks.
Be especially tactful in offering suggestions.
Gently teach some of your critical-thinking skills.
Show acceptance, and praise whatever is worthy.

If the child is a

Accept their suggestions and improvements.
Correct gently and tactfully, as you wish others would.
Recognize your mutual need to express affection.
Show them how to set and reach reasonable standards.
Listen to their criticism without becoming critical.

(Reprinted with permission from *Getting To Know You*, © 2002, Chris Carey (CreativeCommunication Publications)

Adapting And Adjusting Your Style

Whether this graph looks like yours isn't the point. The point is that you've got a "pre-set" personality style. It's how you're wired and it fits *perfectly* in some situations. At other times, your "default setting" may not be the best for a particular situation.

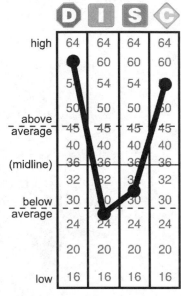

For instance, if you are an insurance broker with 50 agents working for you, this style might work well with very little adjustment. According to this graph, you're task-oriented (**D** and **C** traits are strong), powered to achieve and able to keep track of details. You will probably be a hands-on manager of your workforce and run a tight ship. As long as your work doesn't require you to pass out warm fuzzies to clients who are hit-and-run victims in the local hospital, you might not sense a daily need to become more people-oriented.

But what if your situation changed suddenly — your triplets started medical school at the same time, and to pay college expenses, you took a weekend-and-evenings job at the local pizzeria as Munchie the Clown, making balloon animals for bite-size customers! How well do you think your button-down, no-nonsense approach would work in this scenario? All of a sudden, you would need to adopt a new attitude, tone of voice, posture, standard of dress — your *Pace* and *Priority* would require a major (although temporary and situational) makeover.

This is an extreme example, but every day, situations require us to adjust our styles to serve and accommodate others. Sometimes we do it effortlessly and without thought — like lowering our voices in a library. At other times, we are ripped from our comfort zones and plunged into strange environments. We're forced to do so much bending and twisting in order to meet expectations that we feel like a cross between Gumby and a pretzel. Here are a couple of concepts that can help you manage such transitions.

First, understand that when you are in an environment more suited for your personality style, it's as if your power comes straight from the outlet on the wall — you're plugged in. But your cord can reach only so far, and when you have to stretch far enough, it's as if you must unplug and operate on batteries. Make no mistake about it: Adapting and adjusting uses energy, and you run down faster when you're working out of your zone. You can recharge yourself by doing the things that feed your real needs.

For instance, **D**s may recharge by working out, playing sports, doing something physically active. They may switch gears and work on a challenging new project. Sometimes they instigate change just so they can work on something that requires their active involvement.

Is are "people-people," and being isolated from conversation and freedom to move about drains their batteries quickly. They may leave their desk and visit with coworkers while waiting for the laser printer, because talking and moving around to connect with people is a sure way to charge up again.

While **S**-types are also people-oriented, they would prefer that you visit them if there is any visiting to be done. "Go!" and "Do!" are not motivators for them. A stretch for them is dealing with change, and they may recharge by retreating to the safety and security of familiar places and faces. I've been told that **S**s take more relaxing baths than other styles. Close the door, lower the lights and nurture their souls.

It's tempting to say **C**s don't "do fun" to recharge because it's usually hard for them to waste unfocused time. They are task-oriented and they get charged up checking and correcting things. I think there is a nagging doubt that something is slipping under the radar if they relax themselves or their standards. This is what drains their energy, and what powers them up is getting back into procedures and processes.

Imagine that you are the proud owner of the graph we just looked at. What personality style do you think would work well during your desperate stint as Munchie the Clown?

- Do you see Munchie the Clown as *task-oriented* or *people-oriented*?
- Do you think Munchie should be *slower-paced* and safely predictable, or should this clown be *faster-paced* and impulsive?
- At birthday celebrations, is Munchie's fun lighthearted and silly, or does Munchie appreciate puns and a play on words (to the dubious delight of five-year-olds)?

Learn to "Equalize" Yourself

How would you adjust to fit the Munchie criteria? This visual metaphor will help you: An equalizer for your car stereo controls the highs, lows and mid-range sounds coming through the speakers. If you want more bass and less cymbal-crashing, boost one and lower the other till the mix sounds right to you.

You can also "equalize" your personality style to some extent so the mix sounds right for your environment. If your **D** is a little too "loud" for the situation, turn it down a notch or six. If it's time to pay attention to details, crank up your **C**. Have to deliver those warm fuzzies to the hospital? Bring up your **S** without your **I** getting out of control or the nurses will sedate you!

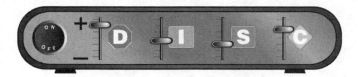

This equalizer is set to match the personality style graph we looked at a few minutes ago. The **D** is near the top, the **I** is below the middle line, the **S** is somewhat lower, and the **C** is almost as high as the **D**.

It would require energy to make a "Munchie" adjustment for a little while, but you know you could recharge your batteries later, so go for it!

- You could pull down your **D** so it's below the midline — not as strong for kids as for your sales team.
- And you could boost your spontaneous, fun-loving **I** enough that the kids would have fun and want to come back again next weekend.
- If you boost your **I** too high, you might overexcite the kids, so remember to raise your **S**, too. This is the part that makes you comfortable and safe for them, and it reassures the nervous moms at the next table.
- And, while you're going to make sure everything Munchie does is carefully thought-out, use your perfectionist **C** to do that beforehand, and then lower it while you're making the balloon animals. So what if the front legs are different lengths? Munchie can make 347 different balloon animals...that all look like doggies!

Square Pegs In Round Holes

We are not "prisoners" of our personality styles. Your style is not a valid excuse for poor choices, poor attitudes or poor actions. Occasionally I hear from a parent whose child has said, "Mr. H says that's just the way I am. I'm a **D** — deal with it!"

It's not so much that *other people* need to learn how to deal with it as that *we* need to deal with it! We're responsible for how we think, behave, respond and relate to others, and our personality styles offer some great tools to work with.

The truth is that your natural style is what it is. Research shows that it pretty much remains constant throughout your life, although we can learn to adapt and adjust.

I think it makes sense to "bloom where you're planted." People who are *task-oriented* have a natural tendency to "stick with the stuff" more than those who are *people-oriented*. Those who need a *faster-paced* environment have a natural tendency to respond to change more readily than those who are *slower-paced*. Since we have special strengths, let's use them well.

As an example, I'm not wired to work alone or handle repetitive details. I can do it, but I don't enjoy it. You wouldn't want me to be your accountant, especially when there are people who really enjoy working with numbers! Instead, I'm wired for fun, inspiration and strategic leadership. Understanding this, doesn't it make sense for me to use my personality style to its full advantage when I'm in a suitable environment? And doesn't it make sense for me to spend less time and effort on the things that work against my style? I shouldn't allow myself to be ignorant or inexperienced in such important areas just because they're outside of my comfort zone. But I'm a round peg and I fit better in a round hole. Finding the right fit is easier on both the peg and the hole!

When Your Only Tool Is A Sledge Hammer

Does this sound familiar to you? It was Dr. Abraham Maslow who said, "When the only tool you have is a hammer, you tend to treat every problem like a nail."

We tend to use tools that are handy, easy to find or close within our reach. I'll bet you have a butter knife in your drawer that has a warped point. You knew it wasn't a screwdriver as you grabbed it, but it was handier, easier to find and closer at hand when you needed to fix something quickly. You used what you had. Sure, you could have dug around in your tool box for the right tool, but this worked okay. You just never put this knife on the table when you have company for dinner.

I thought about **D**-type behavior when I read Maslow's hammer comment. **D**s tend to solve a problem by pounding away until it either breaks or conforms to their desires. I think it's fair to say they tend to do this with people, too.

In *Getting to Know You*, Chris Carey wrote, "Finesse can be stronger than force." This means there are times when a screwdriver can be more effective than a hammer. What we can't accomplish by beating on something may yield to just a twist of the wrist.

The more I thought about hammers, the more I realized that each personality type has a hammer suited to the kind of work they do. Sometimes the hammer that fits well in our hand is not the best one to use for a specific job. We should choose the hammer that gets the job done, not just our favorite one.

I went to *Alspaugh's Ace Hardware Store* in my neighborhood and looked at sledge hammers. You use them for serious construction and demolition. You can drive railroad spikes into cross-ties and knock down walls with this tool.

It's not a "finesse" tool, but it can be the best tool for specific purposes, and other tools can't accomplish what a sledge hammer can. I think of it as a **D**-type tool: massively effective and powerful.

Then I noticed the power hammers nearby. Some are powered by an air compressor and some have a gunpowder charge built into the nail. Either way, their purpose is to quickly connect wood together. Using one is a lot more fun than a regular hammer; it picks up the pace and can make some serious noise. For these reasons, I think of it as an **I** tool.

I was on a roll by the time I reached the mallets! Who would have thought there were so many specialty hammers? You can use a mallet to shape a piece of metal without denting it. Because it operates as a shock absorber, you can also use it to tap a wood dowel into a hole without splintering. Sounds like an **S** tool.

"The problem is the nail. Your perspective is your hammer."

Finishing hammers have a precise purpose. You would really appreciate their design if you were finishing the details on a woodworking project. And carpenters use them on exposed surfaces because they don't nick, chip or dent. Their range of control is very good, so you can use just the right amount of impact to do the job. This, logically, reminded me of the **C** type.

It's not enough to have just *one* hammer; you need the *right* hammer for the *right* job. Even more, you need to know when and how to use each one. Don't try banging away on a spike with your soft mallet unless you want to destroy your mallet. Likewise, there are times when an **S** needs to be more forceful and powerful. There are times when they need to "boost" the **D** on their equalizer. Sometimes you must use sledge-hammer determination and action to move through obstacles. On the other hand, don't use a sledge hammer to drive in a little wooden dowel. That's what mallets are for. Make sure you have the right hammer for the right nail!

The cartoon caption on the previous page says, "The problem is the nail. Your perspective is your hammer!" Don't mistake *someone else's* hammer for *your* nail. By this I mean that another person may not feel it's best to use a sledge hammer when you're ready to start swinging away. Don't pulverize their finishing hammer — it's not a nail! Too often, we oppose people and their methods rather than working together and opposing the problem. As you'll see, knowing your tools and when to use them properly moves us toward becoming *Influencers.*

Chapter 7:
CHOOSING CONTROL OR INFLUENCE

Because I've been teaching high school students until now in my professional career, I've learned to keep my theories and explanations as simple as possible in the beginning. After observing interactions between bosses and employees, teachers and students, parents and children, and husbands and wives.

I've recognized two commonalities in these relationships:
- Leadership is about building relationships.
- Relationships can operate either in *Controller* mode or in *Influencer* mode.

By most modern definitions, we see that great leaders have ability to connect with people.
- Bosses who build solid, mutually beneficial relationships with employees have teams that are more productive and effective.
- Teachers who master the art of connecting with students have classes in which students respect them, listen more and perform better.
- Parents who build solid relationships encourage their children to seek their advice and support.
- Husbands and wives who establish strong relationships are people who count on each other and are best friends.

Yes, I really do believe that great leaders know how to build successful, long-term relationships!

So, in setting up your *Influencer Incorporated* company, how will you choose to run it in order to build long-term, effective, productive relationships? There are two approaches to consider. The first works well if you are looking only for short-term results dependent on constant interaction. If we don't choose otherwise, we default to this approach whenever we want everything to go our way and become closed to others' points of view. I call this model *Controller Limited*.

Controller Limited

Here are two dozen words I've heard from students and adults, describing their feelings and emotions while being controlled by someone else:

- Anger
- Fear
- Not valued
- Used
- Resentment
- Helpless
- Misunderstood
- Shame
- Stupid
- Unloved
- Insecure
- Anxious
- Resistant
- Suffocated
- Worthless
- Abused
- Trapped
- Conflict
- Belittled
- Depressed
- Incompetent
- Unappreciated
- Manipulated
- Taken advantage of

What other words would you use to describe your feelings in a relationship where you have no say-so, no valid input?

In some of my seminars, I drive home this point by asking for audience advice in a make-believe relationship. In this scenario, I say, "I'm dating a girl and want to tell you how she makes me feel when I'm with her. I feel angry, resistant, afraid, suffocated, invaluable, worthless, used, abused, resentful, trapped and helpless. We are in constant conflict. I feel misunderstood, belittled, ashamed, depressed, stupid, incompetent, unloved, unappreciated, insecure, manipulated, anxious and taken advantage of. Do you think I should stay in this relationship?" Of course, they give me that "what a dumb question!" look and say, "No, of course not! You need to get out of that relationship immediately!" Well, *duhhh!*

In presenting this material, I try to be as clear as possible, but sometimes I'm not prepared for what I hear. When I've asked for words that describe relationships built on control, some people have responded, "I feel comforted," or "I feel safe," or "I feel confident." The first time I heard this, I was surprised and at a loss for words. Before I could think about my response, I blurted out, "No, that's not right!" Instantly, the room went icy cold and quiet — people stopped participating. When I told my wife what had happened, she replied, "I guess that lady didn't feel very comforted when you told her that her thoughts weren't valid or important."

I'm pretty sure I lost that relationship the moment I said her point of view was wrong. I've heard such comments many times since, and I've come to understand why someone might use words like "comfort" and "safe." They saw the word "control" and thought "take charge" instead of "dictate."

I'm a take-charge kind of guy — it's part of my style. I'm in the zone when I can be the boss. Unless I am sensitive about it, others may resent me and feel I am attempting to control them. Others have a style (perhaps they have a very low **D**) that welcomes someone establishing a direction they can follow. They feel comfort, safety and confidence that this in-charge person will act with their best interests at heart.

How do you feel when someone takes charge of a situation that requires leadership or insight? If that person is not a *Controller,* you probably feel confident, secure and comforted to know that there is someone willing to take the leadership role. But this is not what I mean when I use the terms control or in control mode. *Controllers* see only from their own perspective. While there may be other viable approaches in a situation, they see only from their own point-of-view and make everyone and everything conform to it.

Most people have no idea when they are coming across in such a way, and they don't want to be corrected if they are! We'll discuss ways to recognize when you have slipped into control mode, but now, let's look at running your company as *Influencer Incorporated* rather than *Controller Limited.*

It's probably wise to say that the *Influencer* approach is much more difficult to develop. It's not just a matter of changing our approach to people, but changing our attitudes about them. It goes against our wiring, whatever our personality style, because we tend to meet our own needs before we think of others. However, becoming an *Influencer* instead of a *Controller* is significantly more rewarding over the long term.

Influencer Incorporated

How would you describe your feelings when you interact or connect with someone who has positively influenced you? What is it to be in influence mode? Here are nearly two dozen phrases people in my seminars have used in describing people who build relationships through influence:

- They genuinely tried to understand me.
- They trusted me and were trustworthy.
- They were open-minded and nonjudgmental.
- They really listened to me.
- They encouraged me.

- They showed me love.
- They appreciated or recognized me.
- They didn't rush me.
- They spent time with me.
- They were consistent.
- They were kind, caring and compassionate.
- They were respectful.
- They were forgiving.
- They were patient.
- They didn't give up on me.
- They didn't judge me.
- They expected a lot me but believed I could do it.
- They held to a standard of right and wrong.
- They were optimistic and positive.
- They were there for me, even when it was inconvenient.
- They were loyal.
- They were passionate and enthusiastic.

What words would you use to describe someone who has influenced you to be better or do more with your life?

Influence, unlike control, requires the ability to keep your own perspective yet, when working with others, seeks to understand their perspective. An on-purpose *Influencer* has a fine-tuned ability to connect with others, believing that relationships should not be one-sided. *Influencers* have learned that, although their perspectives are important, the viewpoints of those around them are, too. I've found no better way to truly connect with people and fully understand their needs, motives and viewpoints than learning and applying the **DISC** personality information.

Parents As Influencers

This book is about influence, not parenting or teaching

children. But it would be a mistake to omit specific information for parents and teachers who want to become *Influencers* in young lives. The following data should provide hope and provoke caution.

A study determined the amount of interaction between fathers and their small children. First, dads estimated how much time they spent each day with their child. Answers averaged 15–20 minutes. Then microphones were attached to the fathers to record each interaction. These middle-class fathers with small children averaged 37 seconds per day of direct interaction: 2.7 encounters lasting 10–15 seconds each!

A Gallup poll in the 1960s revealed the top three influences in a teenager's life were their parents, teachers and spiritual leaders. According to a more recent survey, the top three influences in a teenager's life today are friends, media (music, TV, movies) and parents. Spiritual leaders dropped to number 17 on the list. For practical purposes, they don't exist.

According to *The State of the Nation's Youth 1998–1999*, more than a thousand teens (ages 13–17) were asked, "If you could pick one person as your role model, which of the following categories would your role model be in?" They responded:

- Family members   40.7%
- Friends/family friend   14.4%
- Teaching/education   11.1%
- Sports/sports-related   10.3%
- Entertainment industry   4.9%
- Religious leaders   4.3%
- Business leaders   1.9%
- National political leader   0.5%
- International political leader   0.4%
- Local political leader   0.0%
- Other   11.6%

Although more kids are trying marijuana at an earlier age, parents are convinced that statement doesn't apply to their children, according to a national study by the Partnership for a Drug-Free America. "Boomers, many of whom have 'been there done that,' are surprisingly and ironically out of step with the reality of drugs in their children's lives," Partnership president Richard D. Bonnette said. Studies showed that 60% of boomers had tried marijuana at least once. "Few sincerely believe their children are exposed to drugs or that drugs are widely available in the schools their children attend," Bonnette said.

Their survey was conducted last year with 6,975 teens and 815 parents. Here are the parents' results:

- 43% believed their teens could find marijuana easily. (58% of teens said pot was readily available.)
- 33% thought their kids viewed marijuana as harmful. (18% of teens felt smoking marijuana was risky.)
- 45% felt their teen had a friend who smoked marijuana. (71% percent said a friend had used marijuana.)
- 21% thought their teen could have experimented with marijuana. (44% of the teens said they actually had experimented with marijuana.)

My point is that, just as teenagers are becoming more exposed to drugs, their parents are losing Influence in their lives. Another survey reports that ages 12 and 13 are critical years in the fight against drug use. Few 12-year-olds know how to buy marijuana or know someone who has used hard drugs, but about three times as many do by the time they are 13, according to Columbia University's National Center on Addiction and Substance Abuse.

The survey also found that teens think the drug problem is considerably worse than their teachers, especially their school principals, do. For instance, 78% of teens say their schools are not drug-free; just 18% of principals agree.

This survey concluded that:

- Teens who regularly attend religious services are much less likely to smoke, use drugs, or hang out with people who drink and use drugs.
- Teens who have never smoked marijuana are more likely to eat dinner every night with their parents and to rely on their parents' opinions.
- Pot smokers are more likely to hang out with friends after school and less likely to listen to music or do homework after school.
- Teens who use one substance are more likely to use another; smokers are more likely to drink and use marijuana; pot users are more likely to drink.

When children are small, parents and teachers are their main *Influencers* by default. Radio commentator Paul Harvey told about an 8-year-old named Ben who won a contest at the local McDonald's. His prize was a brand-new bike. When Ben got home, he told his parents that he already had a bike and didn't need two, so he had decided to give his new bike to a friend whose parents were unable to buy one for him. When the McDonald's store manager heard about it, she invited Ben and his family to dinner and presented him with a $100 gift certificate. The next day, Ben used that to buy a safety helmet for his friend.

For some people, giving is just second nature. And the pure heart of an 8-year-old may be a credit to the influence of caring parents. But as a child's world expands, we must compete for the influence we have taken for granted. Sometimes we find it easier just to insist on control. I urge you to continue modeling influence wherever and whenever you can. I love this story, published in *The Readers Digest*, by Roger Craig, former Major League baseball manager and coach:

Once, when I was nine, my dad told me to clean up our garage. When he came home from work, he asked, "Did you take care of the garage?"

"Sure," I replied.

"Let's go see," he said. He took a look around. "Sit down in the corner for a minute," he told me. Then he took off his coat and tie, rolled up his sleeves and started working. I thought I'd done an all right job, but he didn't. "Let me help you," I begged.

"No," he answered, "I want to show you something." He worked about an hour and had that garage spotless.

When he had finished, he said, "I did this so you can remember it all your life. It doesn't matter how much time something takes — if you're going to do it, do it right. Do it the best way you know how."

Even today, whether I'm carrying firewood on my ranch or teaching my pitchers how to pitch, I always think about that.

When I was young, my dad told me no employee would ever have the pride in "our" landscaping business that we did — Hinojosa was its name and ours. It represented us to Houston, and unless a worker's name was Hinojosa, the company name didn't mean anything special to him. I didn't understand as readily as Roger Craig, but as I grew older, I got the message. *Influencers* have to be patient with slow learners!

Former Secretary of Labor Robert Reich was quoted in *USA Today* with this wonderful insight on parenting teenage boys, although I suspect it is as relevant for parents of teenage girls. He said, "Teenage boys are like clamshells. They open up just for a moment in order to take in a little nourishment or expel some dirt. But then they clam up tight again. If you're around when they open up, you have a chance to see something truly beautiful inside. But you have to be there at that moment."

Parents possess unique leverage in passing on respect for family history and the importance of their family's heritage. Next time you or your kids are feeling unimportant, try a little arithmetic trick based on the undebatable fact that it took two people (your biological parents) to get you here. Each of these two parents required two parents, according to the basic birds-and-bees theory, so in the generation just prior to your mother's and father's, four people contributed to your existence. You are the product of:

- 8 great-grandparents
- 16 great-great-grandparents
- 32 great-great-great-grandparents

Continue multiplying by two, calculating an average of 25 years between each generations. You'll see that, 500 years ago, there were 1,048,576 people beginning to produce you — that's a heritage! And somewhere in there, you'll find a lot of influence! We have no idea the potential we leave in our children. "Shakespeare worked without knowing that he would become Shakespeare," according to *Collette, La Jurnelle Noire*. And neither did Shakespeare's mom and dad!

A Bible verse says, "Train up a child in the way he should go; even when he is old, he will not depart from it (*Proverbs 22:6, New American Standard Bible*). Hebrew scholars tell me the passage literally refers to training a child according to his or her unique *bent* — personal style, talents, gifts and identity — and that's what you can do by using this **DISC** information.

An On-Purpose Influencer

As you begin thinking about incidents of influence and control in your life (and especially when you were the control-er and not the control-ee), you may have only begun to see how you imposed your will in order to serve your wants and needs, in spite of what others may have wanted and needed.

We've all done it, so don't imagine my finger waving in your face, with some shrill voice moaning, "Shame, shame, shame on you!" Because we have *controlled* for so long, it's an unconscious habit for most of us. We'll have to consciously unlearn *control* in order to practice unconscious *influence.*

Here's a helpful competency model that may help make this clear: As we learn something new, we have to move first from being unconscious about our ignorance to becoming conscious of our need to learn.

unconscious ➡ conscious

In the beginning, we don't know, and we don't know that we don't know. Whatever information, misinformation and disinformation we rely on isn't enough, but we don't even know enough to know that. So our first step is to be aware that we don't know.

It's pretty good progress just to learn that we don't know what we don't know and that some of what we know isn't so. We move from being unconsciously unaware of our deficiencies to being consciously aware of our sad situation.

Then we should want to do something about it, although it isn't easy to change established patterns or habits. To act differently, we must think differently — consciously! Once we learn how it's supposed to be, we can sometimes (and then, more often) do the right thing and get the result we're after.

We can be competent, with *conscious,* purposeful concentration and effort. But if we get careless, sloppy or forgetful, we fall back into our old ways.

Eventually we establish new patterns, and at some point, they become second nature to us. Then, we're no longer conscious that we've mastered the challenge — we are unconsciously competent!

I see this same pattern at work when we choose to move from *Control* to *Influence:*

unconscious ➡ conscious   conscious ➡ unconscious
CONTROL ➡ INFLUENCE

We can become aware of our own tendencies and preferences — identify our personal behavior style. Then we can begin recognizing when our behavior is appropriate and when it should be restrained or adjusted.

We can take what we're learning about other people and identify their behavioral styles. The purpose here isn't so we can "help" them restrain or adjust what they do. (They'll probably never understand our motives or intentions if we try!) Instead, we can apply what we know about their needs and wants to serve and *Influence* them.

We can begin working on our servant techniques, examining our motivations and actions to see if we're functioning as *Controllers* or as *Influencers.* Frank Warren wrote, "If you wish to be a leader, you will be frustrated, because very few people wish to be led. If you wish to be a servant, you will never be frustrated." This tells me the secret to "welcome leadership" is the kind of influence that serves others.

1	2	3	4	5	6	7	8	9	10

unconscious ➡ conscious   conscious ➡ unconscious
CONTROL ➡ INFLUENCE

No one is looking over your shoulder right now — and if they are, act like a *Controller* and make them go away! Now, seriously look at this graph and circle two numbers:

1. The number that represents where you think you are on the Unconscious *Control* > Conscious *Control* > Conscious *Influence* > Unconscious *Influence* scale. It's possible that at times you are a Conscious *Controller* — on purpose, fully realizing what you're doing, and even choosing not to be an *Influencer.*

2. The number that represents where you would like to find your *Influence* scale. (I emphasized that no one is looking at your scale because this is gut-check time.) Whatever standard you choose to work toward is yours. We'll be looking at standards and consistency soon, because they are parts of the *Influencer* equation. Circle the number that represents an ideal for you. Once you experience how influence works, you'll probably want every interaction to be a *10!*

Recently, I stayed at Bud Hadfield's Northwest Forest retreat in Cypress, Texas. Guests receive a copy of Bud's book, *Wealth Within Reach,* telling about his struggles and successes in founding the *Kwik Kopy* franchise. And it shares many important principles about becoming an *Influencer,* including the poem he has graciously allowed me to reprint on the following page. Thanks, Bud!

Please Help Me

Please come into my life —
but don't try to take over.
Please help me to think —
but don't try to think for me.
Please help me find a better way —
but don't expect me to do it your way.
Please help me — even if I'm wrong.
Help me to stand again —
but don't carry me.
Please help me to move forward again —
even if we move forward
in different directions.
And — last of all —
if you can't help me to be
what I want to be,
then please don't hurt me
by trying to make me
what you expect me to be.
— Bud Hadfield

Chapter 8:
BUILDING YOUR INFLUENCER INC.

Let's get to work on building your *Influencer Incorporated!* You're probably aware that companies must have a balance sheet, a listing of their assets and liabilities. It's amazing that, in a business, companies emphasize their assets (the plus signs) and minimize their liabilities (the minus signs). But individuals tend to see their own liabilities first and devalue anything that might be an asset.

John McCormack, founder of the 16 highly successful *Visible Changes* hair salons spread across Texas, wrote about his experience creating a *personal* balance sheet in his book, *Self-Made in America.* As a young New York police officer, he invested in the stock market, following his hunches, and he became a millionaire. Then he lost it all, plunging hundreds of thousands of dollars into debt when the market crashed.

More than financially ruined, John was personally devastated. As he explains, he thought he had *created* the wave, although he was only *riding* it. Then he met an elderly man named Abe, who, as a mentor, walked him through a process of succeeding with purpose and specific intent. It began with a personal inventory, and all John could list were his liabilities. Abe began asking some basic questions:

- Do you understand a language?
- Do you understand currency?
- Do you know your way around?

When he said he spoke only English, Abe asked if he could read it and write it. John said, "Sure," and was told to list it as an asset. When he said he knew nothing about currency and trading, Abe asked if he could make change for a dollar. If so, write it down! Finally, John said he was street-smart (knew his way around), but Abe asked if he were dropped off on Long Island, could he find his way back to Brooklyn? When John said, "Of course," Abe added that to the assets list, too.

Abe explained that, within a few miles of their meeting, immigrants had recently come to America, not understanding the language, the currency, or even how to find their way around town. Yet several of these immigrants became multi-millionaires in just a few years, with fewer assets and more liabilities than John currently possessed.

Now, what about *you*? You're about to develop a balance sheet for your *Influencer Incorporated* company. (I've referred to it earlier and now you'll create it.) Without looking at finances, list what you see as your resources. Include the strengths you see in your personality style. (When *optimists* look at a glass, they see it as half-full. *Pessimists* see it as half-empty. *Realists* know the glass is going to have to be washed either way!) Are you seeing your assets, your liabilities, or your potential?

What have you learned about yourself from the Personality Style Survey you printed out and completed from the companion CD? There are some struggles attached to your style, as well as some strengths. Perhaps you will include some of those under liabilities. (*But if your liabilities list is longer than your assets list, you need to reread the previous page!*)

Maybe you're so used to being around yourself that it's difficult to make an assets list. Think about what others have said about your skills, talents, abilities and strengths.

Your *Liabilities and Assets* sheet is printed on the next page, and this is the time to begin filling it in. What have you got to say for yourself? *Start writing now!*

How was that as an exercise? If you cut some corners, give yourself some extra time to fill the right column. Parts of this book are supposed to be *s-t-r-e-t-c-h-i-n-g* for you!

How do you remember successes in your life? Did you draw from them when you listed your assets? Most people never "memorialize" their successes (you know, put up a statue to themselves!), so when they experience difficulties, they forget about the challenges they've overcome. Make a note of this:

> **From now on, plan what you're going to do to celebrate and remember even your small successes. They are the signposts to your strengths.**

Your list of assets will be a building block for more to come in this book. Chances are, you've thought of a few more successes that demonstrate your assets. Add them to the list *now*, and then we'll be ready to move on.

What Your Brand Says About You

Your list of assets identifies your company's "products" and "services" — what you do well that your "clients," "customers" and "investors" have interest in. Using your assets brings value to them and increases the worth of your stock.

Your list also includes some liabilities that detract from your brand name's quality reputation. (Too many of these will keep you stuck on the shelf!) You'll want to minimize those liabilities and build "name *appreciation*," as we discussed in Chapter 1.

My Liabilities	My Assets

Think of this as your company's research and development department. Research is one activity (finding out what's available and what's needed) and development is another activity (putting to work what you have learned). Our goal is to help you perform good R&D so you can actually create and deliver what you promise.

Given the personality strengths you have and the assets you listed on your balance sheet, we'll be developing a logo symbol and a slogan that represents your company and the promise it makes to your "customers."

Don't hesitate now! You don't know what you don't know about this process yet. You'll actually enjoy the challenge of identifying ways you bring value and worth to others.

While it's important for a company to be aware of what it does well, it's also important to understand some of its limitations. You're great at some things and you struggle with others. Here's an interesting example to prove my point:

Campbell's Soup is an established brand. Its product is easy to make:

1. Open a soup can.
2. Dump its contents in a pan.
3. Refill the can with water.
4. Pour that water into the pan.
5. Heat it up.
6. Stir it around.
7. Pour it into a bowl.
8. Eat it.

What if someone who worked for *Campbell's* got the misguided idea that, because the directions on their cans were so easy to follow, *Campbell's* should branch out and make road maps with easy-to-follow directions? Based on its assets and experience, is there a good reason customers should trust *Campbell's* as a reliable publisher of road maps? Of course not!

So what's your company's best asset? Remember that *Influencer Incorporated* is more than just *a* business — it's *your* business. Even more, it's your *life!*

Your opportunity is simple: You can choose to provide a great product with great service, because you have *exactly* what someone else is looking for! You have assets that make you uniquely gifted for the pursuit of your dreams, and those assets can take your business to the top!

Imagine that you really do own a business and need to advertise your services to potential customers. A marketing consultant puts together an image and brand, develops a campaign to identify you in the marketplace and puts your message on billboards all over town:

- We can't do anything right!
- We have nothing to offer.
- We have no strengths, just liabilities.
- If you want to see your money wasted, just call us!
- We will absolutely let you down!
- Worst customer service in the city!

Would you hire a marketer who came up with a plan like that? You and I should be concentrating on what we *can* do, but we often focus on what we *can't* do. Even worse, that's what we advertise to others!

Your One Greatest Asset

How often have you told people what you can't do, singling out your liabilities and ignoring your assets? *I would be terrible at this…. I could never do that… I'll never be able to understand that…. I just can't….*

Unlike 99% of Olympic athletes, who spend their lives perfecting athletic skill, my friend Ruben Gonzalez decided at 21 to make his Olympic dreams a done deal — he just needed a sport! Looking through a list of Olympic events, he realized quickly that he wouldn't be able to compete at the Olympic level in any of the Summer Games. So he found one Winter Games sport he could learn: the luge! It's a one-man competition in which athletes slide down an icy track at 80-plus miles an hour.

Why did a Texan like Ruben pick an ice sport like the luge? (This is the part of his story I love!) He recognized one asset that had distinguished him from others throughout his life — just one.

Although Ruben was aware of the things he wasn't able to do, he knew of one asset that could propel him to success: He possessed *single-minded, steadfast persistence and* he would not quit, regardless of the odds or the circumstances!

Ruben's story revolves around his persistence. Experts told him he was too old and said the brutal training caused 9 out of 10 athletes to quit. He could count on pain, broken bones and a beaten body.

He said, "Great!" The harder it was for others to compete, the better his chance to succeed! It would push him mentally and physically, and the faster other athletes quit, the faster he would rise to the top. Ruben's greatest asset was willingness to endure whatever it might take to succeed.

Just like your *Influencer Incorporated* company, Ruben's marketing plan depended on him for success. He was the product and the service. He was his own boss and his own employee. He was both his customer and his supplier. He advertised success to himself with the slogan, "Success: It's A Done Deal!" It became his personal billboard. Soon other people noticed, and they began to believe in his dream, too. His customer service department fulfilled Ruben's promise, "I won't quit until the job is done!"

Ruben Gonzalez's asset propelled him to not one but three Olympic Games over a dozen years! Here's a tip from this three-time Olympian:

Find out what you can do. Then, no matter what, don't quit on yourself and don't quit on your dreams!

I don't know if the following story is true or not, but it illustrates a tendency among people. I've heard that in the late 1800s, a shoe company in England sent a salesman to Africa to sell to scattered tribes. After arriving, the salesman sent a telegram back to his office:

RETURNING HOME. NO ONE HERE WEARS SHOES.

Unaware of the situation, a rival shoe company sent its salesman, who, after arrival, sent back this telegram:

MARKET WIDE OPEN. NO ONE HERE WEARS SHOES.

Are you looking at your assets or your liabilities? What is your singular, greatest asset — the billboard for your company? Remember, it's not something physical or external. Those can be lost, whether they are strength, money or appearance. You have an internal asset already in your possession, waiting to be used, developed and showcased. It's your brand.

Are you still with me? Does it sound too simple to you? Are you still sitting on your *can'ts*? I'm saying that your brand should identify what you do well. Don't dilute it by featuring things you don't do well. When you think and talk about your company (yourself), use powerful, positive descriptions. Believe it or not, you have what someone else is looking for! Everyone has some liabilities, but your assets make you perfect for the life and work that will fulfill your dreams.

ASSIGNMENT: DESIGN YOUR LOGO

1. **Write out your full name. (Example:** BETH ANN WHEELER)

2. **Use your last name as the name of your company. (Example:** WHEELER)

3. **Sketch a symbol or word picture that represents your last name (or what your name means or sounds like). (Example:** A WHEEL)

4. **Using your initials, come up with a phrase that says something meaningful about your USP, your goals or your identity. (Example:** BAW = BECOMING A WINNER!)

5. **Arrange these elements on the next page in a way that appeals to you and reflects the importance of this idea. (See Bethy's example below.)**

EXAMPLE:	**INSTRUCTIONS:**
	As Beth Ann did, follow the instructions and, on page 132, design your own logo and write out what it means to you!

Beth Ann had a stroke of genius that reminds her to "walk her talk." Wheels have spokes, and it's important that the words she "spoke" would make things happen. So she added wheel spokes that would remind her to set the pace and be an example so that when she *spoke,* her words would have *traction!*

One student's initials were M.A.L., and her slogan was "Making A Leader." Mine are A.G.H., and my slogan is "Attitude, Heart, Growth." Beth Ann added "Resources" to her company name, remembering all of her assets. "Becoming a Winner" tells her she is making daily progress toward her goal.

It really doesn't matter how good your graphics skills are, because the real message happens inside your head and heart! What counts is what your logo says to you about your company and your product. For instance, my company that produces my seminars is called Omega Quest, and my company Web site is *www.apurposefuljourney.com.* These words mean something special to me, and I'm a little extra motivated when I say them. They work like magic words on me!

Thomas Watson, Sr., was 40 years old when he became the general manager of a little company that made meat slicers, time clocks and punch-card machines. But he recognized the potential of a machine that businesses could use to process and store information (computers) ten years before they came into business use. He renamed the company "International Business Machines Corporation." Near the end of his life, someone asked when he had realized IBM was going to become such a giant. Watson answered, "Right at the beginning."

Is your logo a worthy representative of you and your assets? Is it a fitting billboard to tell your story? As you grow into a powerful *Influencer,* you'll have more opportunities to introduce the *New and Improved You* to many more customers.

DRAW YOUR LOGO HERE:

Chapter 9:
A ROCK-SOLID FOUNDATION

My friend Don Akers is a professional speaker, but was once a professional boxer of some renown. Once he was repairing a little bridge over a culvert at the entrance to his friend's country property. A small stream running through the culvert had washed it out during a heavy rain. Here's how Don told me the story:

> My friend said, "Just place the washed-out rocks back on top of each other. Then we can shovel some more dirt on top of them and we'll have rebuilt the bridge." I was about to say something about recreating the existing problem when he said, "I know what I'm doing because I had to do the same thing last year."
>
> I thought to myself, "Well, maybe this year, you should do something different!" Although my friend was a genius engineer with impressive degrees, he didn't want to waste his time on this little project.
>
> So when I suggested that we stop and buy some cement to do the job right, he said that if the rain didn't get too bad, these repairs would hold for the rest of the year. I couldn't help thinking that every year, for the rest of his life, he would be replacing his makeshift bridge! He did have one thing right: As long as there was very little rain, he wouldn't have to do a thing. The problem is that, in Texas, it rains very hard every year!

When Don told me this story, I knew I wanted to include it in this book, and I knew I would put it right here because it vividly illustrates how futile it is to live or work without a rock solid foundation. As bystanders, it seems obvious to us when people cut corners or do just enough to get a job done. Life is like school: If you don't do what it takes to pass, you have to take the class again until you get it right.

When I was growing up, my friends and I built and rebuilt a rock bridge from one side of a drainage ditch to the other, as a shortcut for walking to school. It worked great until the heavy rains started, and then it washed out, becoming damaged to the point of uselessness. We never considered that possibility the first time we built it, because the weather was perfect and the bridge worked perfectly, too.

I can still remember the day I walked down to the bridge and it was gone! I was shocked, and there was no time to build another one. I just stood there with my younger sister, muttering, "Well, I guess we're gonna be late." We got better at bridging the ditch, but there was always a storm big enough to ruin our efforts.

Here are some lessons you can apply in running your *Influencer Incorporated* company:

- Life is infinitely tougher to navigate without a rock-solid foundation.
- When you cut corners in life, life has a way of making you go back and do it again.
- You benefit only in the short term by cutting corners.
- *Control* is about taking the shortcuts in life to get what you want. *Influence* is about doing it right the first time and benefiting every time you do it right.
- Sand, dirt and rocks work well enough until rain comes. You don't need a bridge if there's never any trouble.

- Storms always expose bridges that aren't built right.
- Rebuild your bridges every year or every day — or build them right the first time and reap the rewards.
- Most times, you can choose a genuine bridge instead of doing it your way. (Did I mention that just 400 yards away was a real bridge, but we would have had to walk that extra distance going and coming?)

So what about you? What foundation have you chosen to build your life on? When it comes to relationships that last, it's time to build a bridge of influence that connects you to the people you love and work with every day. When your foundation is right and the standard is clear, your bridge stays intact.

Setting Your Foundation

How do we decide what foundation to build on for lasting influence? How can you identify what you stand for, and maybe what you're going to fall for, in life?

When I began teaching this information, I knew that we tend to move toward thoughts that dominate our minds. For instance, I wanted my students to like me. With that thought on my mind, I did and said things to be popular with them. I wanted to fit in at school even though I was the adult! But I had no solid standard on which to base my actions or decisions.

You have probably faced a similar situational dilemma: *What should I do in this situation? Should I go with what I feel? Or should I go with what I've been taught is right?*

When I walked down the hallway and saw a student taking a quiz or working on an assignment, if I thought I could help, I'd lean over and whisper, "The answer's not A, B, or D." When they laughed, I had accomplished my mission — I had connected with a student.

I never thought about consequences; I was just fitting in with students. Then I started teaching this information at my leadership camp and in a class five times a day. That's when I realized how often *what I wanted to feel* got in the way of *what I knew to be right behavior.* My internal conflict got worse as I taught more about character. Quotations stuck in my mind, like:

Character is what you do when no one is looking.

and

It may take a lifetime to create but only a moment to destroy.

I remember the day I walked down a hallway and saw a student sitting at a desk. He said, "Hey, Mr. H! Can you help me real quick?" When I glanced over and saw that he was taking a test, I thought, "He knows asking for 'help' is wrong. He's not asking for *help*; he's asking for the answer."

I could have told him what he wanted to know, but I said this instead: "I'd love to help you out, but that would only help either of us in the short-term." He just stared at me and said, "Okay."

It may seem inconsequential to you, but for me, this was the first time I ever consciously considered the kind of person I was and what I really wanted to stand for (and be remembered for) over my lifetime.

- How do I want my family to see me?
- How do I want my colleagues at work to see me?
- When I go from one place to the next, who am I?
- What standard do I live by?
- Do I make up my own rules as the mood strikes me?
- Am I working hard to "look good and smell good," only to toss away who I am whenever I want to fill some deeper craving?

Living life by a consistent standard provides confidence when you face life's tough questions. As you move away from *Controller* mode toward *Influencer* mode, you'll slowly see every area of your life is being affected.

Wendy influenced me so much because she had a standard she believed in and had lived by since she was six years old. I had always chosen to make up my own standard, whatever benefited me, depending on what I wanted.

The students I see struggling most are in the same battle: *I don't want anyone to tell me what to do! Don't try to fix me — fix yourself!* When someone warns them that their current behavior could cause future pain, they react defensively. *Who are you to tell me? Don't try fix me — fix yourself!*

The good news for me is that I no longer struggle with that battle. I have chosen a standard — a path — that helps me decide *who* I want to be and *how* I want to be remembered. I've found that, by following these guidelines, my life is considerably less complicated and infinitely more rewarding.

You have an assignment coming up: creating a Foundational List called "This Is Who I Am." The adjectives you choose for your list should describe characteristics that last, qualities you would be proud to stand up for throughout your life. Another way of creating your Foundational List is to think about how you would build a strong relationship with someone else. (Here's a hint: Almost everyone writes *Trustworthy* as #1!)

My advice is to stay away from "temporary" characteristics like money, appearance, intelligence, talent/skill, or power and status. However tempting they are, experience shows they do not last. We'll all get older, slower and less beautiful — and there is always someone better and more powerful on the horizon. Concentrate on what you can *do*, not so much on what you *want,* to develop a foundation you can stand on during good times and bad. You'll also find that placing these characteristics on your list will help you to get what you want!

Special Note: Depending on your personality style, you will look at each characteristic a little bit differently. Be aware of your definition when you write down each quality or trait. **D**s tend to define trust differently from an **I**, an **S**, or even a **C**. So there is no confusion, you can look up the real definition of each characteristic. You're creating a list of ideals. Even though trust is critical to building effective, long-term relationships, we often fall short of our ideal. This doesn't mean the ideal itself is flawed; it means we must work consistently to attain and maintain it.

Companies, as well as people, make mistakes. Being able to say, "We fell short of our ideal, but we're working on a better product for you every day" keeps them in business. A company that falls short of its ideal and says, "This product doesn't meet our standards, but were saving money at your expense" will fall under scrutiny and eventually go out of business. As owner of your *Influencer Incorporated,* you face this same choice everyday:

Try breaking principles and they will break you!

I've learned that I can wander away from the ideal standard for only so long. The more I deviate, the more I make selfish decisions and the more my relationships falter. If I continue, it isn't long until the principle I am ignoring breaks me.

What does "breaking me" look like? Let's continue using trust as an example. Choosing to lie to someone about where I'm going or what I'm doing may have no short-term consequences. But as I continue to lie and move away from the standard of trust, I inevitably create lack of trust. In the short-term, I break the principle but, ultimately, the principle catches me — the game is up and I'm known as a liar. Whatever was gained short-term is lost, and the result is that the standard of trust exposes me for what I am: a liar who is not to be trusted.

So *your* Foundational List really represents how you want to run your *Influencer Incorporated* company. Fine-tune it using a clock, a birthday cake, and a map to represent key questions you should ask yourself:

 ## Is This Characteristic Time-Sensitive?

Whether it's morning, noon or night, the characteristics you have chosen should be appropriate and work well all the time. You need to be trusting in the daylight and also in the dark. Have you noticed that, as the day goes by, some people leave behind more of their Foundational Lists? Business and personal are as different as day and night? "Well, it's night-time — time to party! It's nighttime — time to break the rules!"

 ## Is This Characteristic Age-Sensitive?

Whether you're 15 or 55, you should be trustworthy. Age is no excuse to go against your Foundational List. You don't magically become responsible at 21. You're responsible always, and 21 is just your birthday! It is your responsibility to decide how you will live as you get older.

 ## Is This Characteristic Location-Sensitive?

This is the biggie! Many of my students want to adjust

their Foundational List according to their location. When they're at home or around an authority figure, the foundational qualities seem right and important. But when teens leave their homes, schools or areas that have real rules and boundaries, they want to forget their foundation and make their own rules.

A classic example is Spring Break. Why do you think so many young people leave town, even going to other countries, to "enjoy" Spring Break? Their answer: "I can change my rules in Mexico. I don't have to think about what's right."

Either your Foundational List is good or it isn't! Just because you go somewhere else, should you really be less honest, less trustworthy or less responsible? Wherever you go, take your Foundational List with you! I tell my students — and you, too, if you will listen:

> **You will never regret what you *stand* for!**
> **You will often regret what you *fall* for!**

- Where do you stand when it comes to the tough decisions in your life? Do you buckle under pressure or do you stand up for what you believe?
- Why is it so easy to talk about trust and respect, but so hard to actually follow through in all areas of your life?
- If you value trust, why would you ever settle for less in yourself and in others?
- Why do you practice such characteristics in some areas of your life but neglect it in others?

In his book, *Life Is Tremendous!,* Charles "Tremendous" Jones explains that the Law of Use and Disuse is at work in your life, just as it is in nature. What doesn't get exercised and used withers away. This means if you actually value *Trustwor-*

thiness and want it to grow stronger, you have to use it. If *Integrity* is on your list, it grows stronger as you exercise it and weaker as you ignore it.

Your Foundational List is so important for your success — it's time to stand for something before you fall for everything! *Take the time now to create your Foundational List. It's too important to think about doing it later!*

All you're going to need is a pen and paper. Write the words "This Is Who I Am" at the top of the page, and then the numbers 1 through 11 down the left side. Fill in the list with qualities you believe should be part of every person's foundation. If you agree with me, write *Trustworthy* in the first line. Then fill in nine more characteristics — leave #11 blank for now. (Later on, you'll prioritize your list, but now you're just "thinking on paper" and neatness *doesn't* count. Go!)

If you've finished the assignment, you have one line left to write. For #11, write these words: *Under Construction.* This means none of us is perfect — including you! By writing this, you're giving yourself permission to *become* the person you described on your paper, even though you're not there yet and won't always live up your ideal.

Notice that you haven't given yourself permission to break any principles, but you have given yourself permission to get better. We all have areas in our Foundation that need to be cleared off and cleaned up! Keeping your Foundation strong is a never-ending process. Don't get discouraged — remember that you and I are always *under construction!*

Here is my own "This is Who I Am" list as I've developed it over the past three years. It's still a work in progress, and it has grown from 11 characteristics to 16! Your own list will continue to be a work in progress, too. If it helps, you can add to it, keep it, or toss it and create one that's totally original. Focus on what you *believe in* and what you *stand for!*

THIS IS WHO I AM

1. *Trustworthy — I am faithful, honest and genuine.*
2. *Special — I have a purpose for my life. I am wonderfully unique.*
3. *Compassionate — and filled with a passion for life.*
4. *Energetic — and enthusiastic.*
5. *Willing to listen — and willing to learn.*
6. *Loyal — and reliable.*
7. *A person of integrity — and character.*
8. *Dedicated — I am persistent, patient and committed to what I say and do.*
9. *Supportive — and respectful to everyone.*
10. *Responsible — and prompt in keeping my commitments.*
11. *Consistent — in forgiving and making healthy decisions for my life.*
12. *Teachable — and authentic. I am willing to grow.*
13. *Optimistic — I see struggles as opportunities and setbacks as chances to learn.*
14. *Willing to understand — to see others' perspectives and to leave this world a better place.*
15. *A person of my word — I keep the promises I make to others and myself!*
16. *Under Construction!*

Make the time to create your own list. When you're satisfied, put it on your mirror. Read it three times a day, and you'll be surprised how the way you see yourself begins to change. If your list is too long, don't worry about eliminating something important. Instead, prioritize and concentrate on the top 7 you want to work on now — you can work on more later. You'll become more aware of the characteristics you write down, and *you can become the person on your list!*

This story demonstrates why your foundation is even more important than your talents. A man named Emmanuel Ninger was arrested for passing counterfeit $20 bills. During a search of his home, police found a $20 bill in the process of being printed.

They also found three watercolor paintings by Emmanuel Ninger. He was an excellent artist — so good that he had hand-painted those $20 bills, meticulously, stroke by stroke, he had fooled everyone, until the wet hands of a grocery clerk exposed him. After his arrest, Ninger's three watercolors were auctioned for $16,000 — over $5,000 each!

The irony is that it took him almost the same time to paint one $20 bill that it took him to paint a $5,000 portrait. This talented man was a thief in every sense of the word, stealing the most from himself. Not only could he have marketed his talents legitimately, but he could have brought joy and benefit to many. Instead, he chose to compromise his integrity. The expression is true: When you break a principle, the principle breaks you.

Finally, if you're tempted to move on or have already decided to skip making your Foundational List, read the note on the following pages. I received it from one of my students last year. It's not at all about me — it's about her, as she shared how her "This is Who I Am" list changed her life.

Mr. H,

As I look back on the past 18 weeks, I realize that my participation in the most unique class I've ever taken (covering life, growth, who you are, the decisions you make and, who you want to be) concurred with some of the most powerful, scary, detrimental, struggle filled, transitional, and important 18 weeks of my life. What a coincidence!

You know what, the first couple days of your class, I arrogantly believed that I would understand the things that you were teaching more than any other girl in that room. I thought that they would listen, but not truly comprehend. I thought that I was so far ahead of the game because I had a lot of life experience, and the class is essentially about life.

I see now that I was wrong. I came to realize that my familiarity with personal life experiences did not put me ahead, but behind; behind because many of those experiences were negative.

I had no foundation, a pessimistic attitude and lots of other setbacks. Many of my classmates already knew what you were talking about, because they live by that standard every day. The truth is that maybe they didn't need to understand as much as I did, because maybe they were already there. I failed to recognize that yes, you do learn from the negative things that happen in life, but if you are not careful, you learn the wrong lessons, completely corrupting your belief system (I think you used the term "bad beliefs").

Many people say that you get stronger when you go through tough times, but again, if you are not careful, all that you become is harder on the outside, and weaker on the inside, and people often tend to label that as "strength", when they are two totally different things.

So, when I ask myself what I learned, as you challenge me with the task of summing up the past 18 weeks, the first thing that comes to mind is that I realize I don't know everything. I shouldn't have been so arrogant to think that I knew more than everyone else because I've had more struggles. If I'm the one struggling in life all the time, I am, most likely, the one who has more learning to do. I see now that when the wrong things are happening, it is very difficult for me to learn the right lesson. I will make the supposition, because I cannot say first hand, that when you do right, you will always learn the right thing, and will have less to hold you back.

Moving along...I proved to myself; through unfortunate experience, a very important point you emphasized in class. I truly learned, that if you don't know who you are, if you don't know what you stand for and lack a foundation, you are also empty, weak, prone to do wrong, and willing to go wherever the wind takes you.

Because I never believed I could ever be all of those positive things, when we first started talking about foundations, I didn't buy into the idea. The way I thought caused me to completely overlook something truly imperative to how you live your life.

One night, when I was in the midst of a very depressed, confused and emotional episode, I was looking through my papers, and I found my "This Is Who I Am" list. When I started reading it, I actually got a little teary eyed. I don't really know why, but it showed me how far away I was from being all those things. I realized if I became somewhat distraught by that idea, it must be important to me after all. I guess I actually do care about it, or else the mere sight of a piece of paper wouldn't bother me so much. I have always fallen, because I was never standing on anything in the first place.

If I truly wanted to, I could list thousands, but I'll talk about something else with which I tended to struggle. When we discussed the four basic people needs in class, my mind raced. I already knew about those basic things, I just didn't like to think about them. I can look back at my behaviors and actions and trace many of them to my own unfulfilled needs. I thought about every drug I've taken, every time I've gotten drunk, every time I've had sex, all of my crazy, emotionally destructive fits of venomous rage, tears, and confusion (I have these little episodes sometimes...it's really nothing). I can pick out details of my life, and say, "I did that to cover up my feeling of this. I did this because I believed that. And that bad belief came from my attitude and the way that I think, which developed from letting some outside conflict change me on the inside just because I didn't have a foundation strong enough to challenge the things that hurt me."

And when you dig down deep, to what the real problems are, not the behaviors that tell you they exist, the truths about them are so simple. By that I mean, the external problems are always complicated, and twisted, and hard to understand, but underneath all the mess, everything is so simple:

"She is insane... she has no morals... she continuously steals... she makes herself throw up... she does cocaine every night... she hates her parents... she always fights with her friends... she slits her wrists... she sleeps around... she yells and screams, and curses God and everyone else, and trusts no one...she doesn't feel loved...."

Sometimes it is just that simple, painful, but simple.

Everything ties together: who you are, how you think, your attitude, your needs, your behaviors, your foundation, how you work with others, your personality — it makes sense, it works, it's the truth.

When you lose control of life and everything falls apart, and the mess becomes so intoxicatingly thick that it suffocates and hides the truth inside, you reach a point where you have to step back, and think long and hard about everything you think you know and believe, gain some perspective, and decide that this time is the last time you let yourself hit the floor.

It isn't easy, it takes time, it hurts, but you know what? Looking in the mirror and seeing the scars on your face from hitting the cold, sharp, hard, bottom doesn't hurt any less.

Little by little, we learn. I learned maybe this time, I will move on, believing something that won't hold me back, something that will help.

This is my answer to your question: "What did you learn?"

I am trustworthy and confident
My mind is clear and I am open-minded
I am determined and motivated
Healthy and strong willed
I have inner strength
I am brave
I will not settle
I am wise
Sincere
I am a winner
I am enthusiastic and energetic
I have character
I am compassionate
I am optimistic and disciplined
Reliable
I have inner strength
And desire
I have a dream
I use my time wisely
I have passion
I am goal oriented
And grateful
I finish what I start

Chapter 10
KEYS TO INFLUENCE

Most people are not out to get you; they are simply looking out for themselves. A key to building influence with individuals is increasing our understanding of each type's preferences and tendencies — how people see their world and what makes them comfortable.

When I crawl in from my business commute in the evening, my children don't run up to me, arms reaching and lips puckering, with the intention of annoying me. They're excited to see me and want a hug and a kiss, even if unwinding for a few minutes feels like a priority to me on some days. Which needs adjusting to increase my influence, their priority or mine?

Many conflicts are a result of misunderstanding people:
"I thought you hated me."
"No, I thought you hated me."
"I thought you said you were going to take care of this."
"But I thought you were!"
Misunderstandings lead to conflict and more misunderstanding. People don't have it *out* for you, they have it *in* for themselves! If you're struggling in relationships, others may think it's because you have it out for them. Gaining influence is about seeing from others' perspectives and acting on their behalf as well as your own.

Each **D**, **I**, **S** and **C** type has ideal environments, communication styles and motivators. Just by seeking to understand these types and how they see the world will improve your capacity to influence them.

Here's a for-instance: My father is one of the most goal-oriented, positive men you could ever meet. As a boy, I heard him say hundreds of times, "Son, you are not average. You will never be average. You don't think like the average person, and that's why you'll never do average things!" I got the message and figured that I wasn't meant to do average things.

My parents were good providers; my sisters and I had all of our material needs met. However, around 13 or 14, I started feeling that whatever I did would never be good enough to earn my dad's approval and praise:

"You missed that spot."

"You could have done that like this."

"If you'd taken your time, you could have done it better."

It seemed that his mission was reminding me how imperfect I was, making me feel incompetent about everything I did. If he and I had understood personality styles and differences, we would have realized what was happening, but his communication and my interpretation created an ever-widening gap between us.

According to Abraham Maslow and others, there are several needs every human has, regardless of personality style:
- **Safety and Security** — a sense of protection
- **Love** — usually connected in a sense of mutual understanding and acceptance
- **Value** — recognition, appreciation and self-worth
- **Purpose** — contribution and importance; providing some value through who I am

Each style has additional needs. My strong **I** was looking for recognition, approval, popularity and attention. My dad's strong **C** wanted quality, attention to detail and excellence. We didn't see eye-to-eye even when I mowed the lawn! I began cutting our one-acre yard with a push mower — not a pleasant task for anyone, just a necessary chore. My dad always found the spot I had missed. So I became extra careful, only to hear, "You didn't miss any spots this time, but you cut the grass so low, you're going to burn it up."

When he told me what was wrong, I felt rejected and useless. "You missed that spot" sounded to me like, "I can't stand you. Can't you do anything right?" So I stopped listening to him and looked elsewhere for approval. My dad's **C** style noticed details that needed correcting, and excellence — if not perfection — was his goal. But my goal was recognition, and I wanted to hear him say, "Son, you worked hard and I'm proud of you. You are the greatest lawn boy in the world!"

Wouldn't it be great if the people we care about most understood our needs best? If we had known this when I was a teenager, we would have been buddies then, as we are now.

Let's look at commonly listed factors when I ask teens and adults to descibe people who have been major *Influencers* in their lives. I most often hear these:

- Trusting and Trustworthy
- Encouraging
- Patient
- Consistent and Loyal
- Nonjudging
- Loving
- Involved
- Forgiving

They Trusted Me And Were Trustworthy

If I say again that influence begins with trust, I'm going to sound like a broken record. There must be some level of credibility for someone to be influenced by what you think, say or do. There can be no real true connection or influence without a degree of trust. Each personality type has a different perspective about it:

- **D**s protect themselves by seeking control. When they give trust, they expect a great deal in return and are very sensitive to being taken advantage of.
- **I**s are very trusting, sometimes even gullible to their detriment. They begin with optimism, thinking people are great and everyone should be trusted.
- **S**s take time to open up, but once they have shared trust, they are extremely loyal, sometimes enabling people to misuse their relationship.
- **C**s take time to reveal themselves. Because of their critical, questioning nature, they need to see demonstrated, consistent action that proves trustworthiness.

They Were Open-Minded And Didn't Judge Me

People who listen and don't seem judgmental can build influence by seeking to understand. "Teachable" is the opposite of knowing it all. This doesn't mean agreeing with every action, behavior or belief, just being willing to look objectively at facts and feelings and compare them to your standard.

Young people often go to friends for advice because they feel less likely to be judged. As parents, we want the best for our children, and remaining open-minded to let others talk and share their view is part of "winning the right to be heard" by them. This is especially hard when we discuss values or moral issues. The more we can at least hear how they see the world, the better our chances of connecting with them. I've learned to *at least* listen to what others say so we will have a *next time* to talk. Otherwise, young people (and many adults) feel personally rejected along with their ideas. When people feel we are judging them and either can't or won't see the world as they see it, we lose our ability to influence them positively.

They Encouraged, Appreciated And Recognized Me

I've heard that Teddy Roosevelt always thanked and encouraged people around him. During campaign trips, he would leave his private train car to thank engineers and firemen for a safe and comfortable journey. It required only moments of his time but earned him friends for life.

I was a summer intern at my church, working daily with our senior pastor. After I had explained my work with personality types, he asked me to add some **I** "flair" to his sermon notes. At the end of the week, I sat down with him, his newly written sermon in my hands. From his leather chair, he took my notes, read the first line and then fell out of the chair, rolling and howling on the ground! I was astounded! I exclaimed, "Pastor, what are you doing?" He looked up and said, "Just giving you a lot of recognition, like your style needs. This sermon is great!" I would follow my pastor right into the pits of hell because he did something very few people have done — he recognized me according to my style! He met me where I was at. Really amazing from a man who has a powerful **D-C** style!

Imagine walking down a street and seeing a row of four shops, each with a big sign reading "Get Your Encouragement Here!" The **D** store's automatic door would spring open when you walked up. You would immediately be told that you are in charge and be given options to do whatever you would like. Everyone would wait for your direction and follow your decisions. The staff would be present and on call but out of your way. The newest and best products would be available.

Next door, the **I** store would have music, confetti and a group of cheerleaders to celebrate your arrival. Your name would be up in lights and everyone would agree that you are the funniest and cleverest person in the world. They would listen attentively to your stories and be impressed with all of your accomplishments. They would never want you to leave and would send you off with a huge party.

As expected, the **S** store would be located conveniently and would have already sent its customers a special note explaining the store's layout and how much they want you as their satisfied customer. They would allow you to look around at your own pace, without pressure to buy, and would show appreciation by keeping in touch even after you left the store.

The **C** store would greet you with a cost comparison sheet validating why you should shop with them. It would be clean, efficient and staffed with knowledgeable salespeople who would value you as a savvy consumer. Before you left, they would ask you to complete a customer service questionnaire so they could run the store more efficiently.

They Showed Love, Kindness, Caring, Compassion, Respect

According to Gary Chapman's book, *The Five Love Languages*, there are five ways by which others speak to our hearts: time, acts of service, words of encouragement, physical touch, and gifts.

I believe we have our personality love languages as well, connected to what makes us feel recognized or appreciated. What has dramatically improved my love for my family is that I *first* committed to understand their personality styles and *then* began working to *show* how much I love them every day. This act of influence is, by far, the most demanding, especially if you're trying to show love to someone you're not getting along with who is causing you pain. A friend explained it to me this way:

"My wife needs love like a river needs water. When I withhold love, kindness, compassion and care, the river dries up. I have the ability to release a flow of love anytime, but I hold onto it and the riverbed starts to crack and lose its life. I turn on the water sporadically and see very little change because the riverbed can't thrive with so little water. When I keep the water flowing continually it starts seeping in and creating a rich stream."

Even the driest riverbed, given enough water, can flourish again over time. How much love did you release when you first believed your spouse was the love of your life? How much have you released today? In *The Passionate State of Mind*, Eric Hoffer offered these insights:

> **The remarkable thing is that when we really love our neighbor as ourselves, we do unto others what we do unto ourselves. We hate others when we hate ourselves. We are tolerant toward others when we tolerate ourselves. We forgive others when we forgive ourselves. It is not love of self but hatred of self which is at the root of the troubles that afflict our world.**

They Were Patient And Didn't Rush Me

I've heard that "patience is something you admire in the driver behind you, but not in the one ahead of you." Patience demonstrates that we don't have to be in control of everything, that we can accept a pace that is different from what we prefer, that we can value other priorities.

I like the old word for patience: long-suffering. Showing that you are on someone's team, even when things aren't going well, may require that we suffer a long time! Patience is one of the greatest tools of *Influencers.* Demonstrating patience means adapting to the pace of people you work with. How does this happen specifically?

- **D**s need you to be patient as they learn to be more understanding and less demanding of others. They also need your patience as they work on letting go of their need to control every situation.
- **I**s need you to be patient as they continue to work on focus and priorities. They also need you to be patient as they work on thinking more about you and less about themselves in conversations.
- **S**s need your patience as they work on standing up for themselves and adapting to changing environments. They also need you to be patient as they learn to stand up and speak up for themselves.
- **C**s need your patience as they work on finalizing details and collecting facts for their projects. They also need you to be patient as they work on being less perfectionist and critical of themselves and others.

They Spent Time With Me, Even When It Was Inconvenient

A mom told me that, even when she was with her daughter, she wasn't really *with* her daughter. We were talking about cellphones when she said she had once looked forward to the time she and her daughter spent in the car after school. "Now," she said, "I've become so busy that I spend that time on my cellphone to be more efficient. I get a lot done, but I don't talk to my daughter in the car anymore. I'm with her, but I'm not *with* her."

Students have told me their parents are home but not *at home* — present in the house, but without time for their children. It's a sign of the times. In a restaurant, I saw two teenage girls sitting together. When one received a call, she answered and didn't stop talking for 30 minutes. Her friend ate, left for 20 minutes, came back, and the other girl was still talking away.

A young mom was devastated when her five-year-old daughter approached her while she worked obsessively with her award-wining roses. The little girl tapped her on the shoulder and asked, "Mommy, do you think you'll ever love me as much as you love your flowers?" People believe we spend time with what we value most. Robert Brault said it well:

> **I value the friend who for me finds time on his calendar, but I cherish the friend who for me does not consult his calendar.**

They Were Consistent And Loyal

We become known by the consistency of what we say and do. I get excited about parents who want to show their children how much they mean to them after attending one of my seminars. When their plan doesn't work as they expected, some parents let me know that "my technique" doesn't work. I ask how often and for how long they continued in their efforts.

"Oh, I did it right away, as soon as I came in the door! I told him, 'You and I need to spend more time together.' And I'm telling you, he just walked off, shaking his head like I was crazy!" People believe consistency rather than conversation.

Here's another example: Some parents "consistently" lecture (over and over and over!) about the same subject without achieving their desired outcome. I advised a father to tell his daughter he loved her *every* day. "But she still doesn't talk to me," he replied. I predicted, "After about two weeks, she'll at least realize you're saying you love her *just because*. It might take another month or two, or even a year, for her to realize that they're not empty words but have real meaning."

Whether positive or negative, when we consistently practice a behavior, people begin to believe it's how we feel. Consistently negative impressions have to be overwritten with more consistently positive impressions so what you really want them to know and feel becomes true.

Think of a restaurant where you've been eating for more than a year. Can you draw correlation between the consistency of that restaurant (perhaps its quality of service, products, price and value) and what people look for in their relationships?

- How have they treated you?
- When serving you, how have they spoken to you?
- What has been the quality and consistency of the food?
- What about the atmosphere?
- How about their pace in accommodating your needs?

Are you getting the picture? We go to places where we feel welcomed and understood, and we keep going back when that experience is consistent.

For me- this is LeRoy's Great Bear

They Were Forgiving And Didn't Give Up On Me

As a kid, when I complained about people, my dad always said, "Nobody's perfect!" I thought, "Well, why doesn't *Nobody* go hang out with *Somebody Else* then?"

If we want a relationship to survive and thrive, we must be willing to forgive people. The act of forgiving shows that we know we're not perfect and don't always have to be in control. Influence grows when we're able to set aside our pride, admit that our actions have wounded another person, and then humble ourselves to ask for forgiveness and set things right. And if we are the wounded ones, we have to be willing to extend forgiveness.

Each of the four basic personality types tends to use a different approach when they must apologize. Some approaches are more effective than others, depending on the syle of the individual hearing their apology:

D: "Sorry, but is was partly your fault. Okay, I will say I'm sorry as long as you say it at the same time." (They want an exchange so they are in no one's debt.)

I: "I'm sorry. Please forgive me." (They may want to spend the rest of the day doing fun things with you, making sure you still like them.)

S: "I am truly sorry. I didn't mean to." (**S**s seldom hurt others' feelings intentionally. They want the conflict to be over and really want you to know how sorry they are.)

C: "Procedure is procedure, and I know I did it right." (Don't wait for a tear-filled, heart-felt apology. From their perspective, procedures failed, not them personally.)

When **D**s and **C**s believe they've been wronged, they are pretty hard on whoever owes them an apology. Often, the *result* of causing a **D** to lose power, or causing a **C** to lose quality, is seen as more offensive than the *action* itself.

I've seen devastating outcomes when **D**s and **C**s withhold forgiveness from **I**s and **S**s. *Task-oriented* types tend to be more interested in the mechanics, while *people-oriented* types are more interested in the relationship. If you are *task-oriented*, think more about feelings than logic when apologizing to or forgiving a *people-oriented* individual.

The late comedian Buddy Hackett used to say, "Never carry a grudge. While you are, the other fella's out dancin'!"

When thinking about commitment and not giving up, I enjoy this essay by American scholar/pastor William Arthur Ward:

For This One Hour

For this one hour, I can be grateful. I can thank God for life itself, for opportunities, for friends, and for a hundred other blessings and privileges to be counted, cherished, and enjoyed.

For this one hour, I can be cheerful. Equipped with a smile, a song, and a sunny disposition, I can transform the atmosphere, enrich my environment, and brighten the day for others.

For this one hour, I can be optimistic. Striking a happy medium between the pessimist and the Pollyanna, I can realistically and confidently expect good things to happen to me and through me.

For this one hour, I can spend some time in prayer. I can pause to recharge my spiritual batteries, renew my mental perspectives, refresh my physical energies, and replenish my faith in God and my fellow man.

For this one hour, I can be unselfish. I can take the Golden Rule off the shelf, dust it, unwrap it, and put it to work in my thoughts, words, and actions right now.

For this one hour, I can look for the best in others. It may take some diligent searching, patient seeking, and careful screening, but I will work at it, even as I want others to look for the best in me.

For this one hour, I can help make someone happy. I can do it through a word of encouragement or comfort, or perhaps by a helping hand, an understanding touch, an empathetic look, a telephone call, a letter, or a visit.

For this one hour, I can be forgiving. I can leave the lowlands of resentment, grudges and bitterness, and rise to the highlands of understanding, love, and forgiveness.

For this one hour, I can be generous. I can listen quietly and attentively when others want to talk. I can look for opportunities to give a well-deserved compliment to someone who needs it most.

For this one hour, I can live in the present. Now is the only time I have, and I can use this hour wisely as a personal and precious gift from God.

— William Arthur Ward

Chapter 11
WHAT WE KNOW
AND WHAT WE DO

I love the story about the revival preacher whose sermon was drawing many shouts of approval from the "Amen Corner" at the church. The more he condemned sin, the louder they hollered, until he got to the sin of gossip. Then the crowd became strangely quiet. He thought maybe he'd been misunderstood, so he repeated himself. No response. He yelled, "Can I get a witness?" And someone spoke up: "Preacher, you done stopped preachin' and started meddlin'!"

Pardon me if I meddle, but unless we *apply* what we know about personality styles, people, control and influence, none of it will really matter. Are you seeing how they play out in your workplace and home? When you and I are in positions of power, it's easy to fall into selfish *Controller* mode and neglect the power of being an *Influencer.*

We're going to visit your Foundational List again, and this time, we're looking at *consistency* as a key to influence. Albert Einstein said:

> **Try not to become a man of success, but
> rather try to become a man of value.**

In order to influence, we must live according to qualities that provide guideposts to success and significance, no matter what events or circumstances occur in our lives.

No one I've met has written "controlling others" on their

Foundational List of principles to live by. Instead, many have said we should draw a big circle around the list and then write the word "consistent."

Consistency makes the difference. *Become* the qualities and characteristics on your Foundational List and be consistent about them. *Consistently become trustworthy!* Consistently show compassion and respect for others! Consistently take responsibility for your actions and behaviors! Your employer, colleagues, friends and family know you by what you do again and again and again!

Sometimes people get frustrated when they hear a good speech, sermon or motivating talk. They are "influenced" to put an idea into practice...for about 60 seconds. Then they say, "I knew it wouldn't work. That guy doesn't know what he's talking about!" Taking your Foundational List for a spin around the block, to see how friends and family like it, won't bring you the results you're looking for. To the contrary, influence is a life-long pursuit of learning and growing.

Earlier, we discussed conscious versus unconscious influence. We're not even aware whether our unconcious behavior is *Influencing* or *Controlling,* because we do it consistently. Conscious behavior requires a deliberate choice. Making the transition requires us to consciously choose to do so.

How About A High-Five?

Through consistency, my Friday classes have developed a tradition I call the Weekend High-Five. My students know to wait for me to get to the door so I can tell them to have a great weekend and get my high-five hand slap as they leave.

When I first started teaching, I wanted my students to know that I cared about them outside the classroom. I promised that I would say Hi and expect a high-five, even in the hallway. They didn't take me seriously until the first time I did what I had promised.

I didn't think much of it until I received a note from a young man who wrote, "Mr. Hinojosa, I want to tell you how much I appreciate your giving me all those high-fives over the year. You will never know how much that meant to me. I hated school and felt lonely, but I could always count on you to brighten up my day."

Since then, I have continued to reach out to my students and the Weekend High-Five has been a way to show them I care. Every day, another teacher at my school tells his students, "You be careful. Have a great day!" It doesn't sound like much in print, but he's having a huge impact on his students. Influence doesn't have to be something big and important; it can be small and significant.

Another student slept every day in my leadership class. He would come in and immediately put his head down to catch some zzz's. And every day, without exception, I would tell him to pick his head up and participate in class. After a month, he said, "Mr. Hinojosa, I'm a graduating senior, and I'm not going to give you any more than this! You should be happy because I sleep 100% of the time in my other classes, and I only sleep about 40% in yours." That didn't make me feel better.

I didn't give up and continued inviting him every day to participate fully. Since he was heavily into weight lifting, I asked him, "What if you needed 100% of your strength to lift the weight but you only gave it 40%? Would you get the weight up?" It didn't phase his attitude or his participation.

I have learned to never give up on students, even when they've given up on themselves. If I promote a certain attitude and don't do it consistently, they let me know I'm not living up to my own standards. It's tough talking about character and positive attitude when I'm having a bad day!

It was a particularly bad day when I learned that my close friend had committed suicide. Even my nonparticipator noticed I wasn't my normal self. They asked what was wrong, so I told the class about my friend and shared a personal story about my own struggle with self-esteem.

The next day, this noninvolved student wrote to me that he knew what I was going through; if I ever needed to talk, he would be there. He explained that he had experienced a loss from suicide as well. He found his mother dead and she had not told him goodbye. I realized why he had given up on people who talk about what life can become, how great things are, and going for your dreams. He saw me as just another person who would eventually let him down. From that point on, he saw me differently and treated me differently. My consistency had worn him down and my openness about my feelings and care for others gave him a sense that I could be trusted. Never give up on people — be a great influence in their lives!

Positive And Negative Trigger Spots

At some point, I think every boy imagines being a professional athlete. Basketball was one of my favorite sports. I practiced for hours every day, perfecting my shooting. Certain "sweet spots" on the court were really good for me. If you asked me to play a game of H-O-R-S-E, I could go right to one of my spots and make baskets again and again.

When I teach students how the mind works, I ask what "their spot" is. I tell them that when they shoot from their spot, they expect to succeed; their mind, body and expectations all line up. They "see" themselves making the shot and they aren't surprised when they do.

If they miss, they shoot until reality lines up with their expectation. Their self-talk sounds like a coach, not a critic: "Now that wasn't like me — I never miss from my spot! Give it to me." Again and again and again, until "Yesssss! I made it!"

I avoided other spots on the floor. Full of doubt, my mind and my muscles responded accordingly. I expected to fail and wasn't surprised when I did. My inner critic told me I was no good from this spot: "You always miss from here — you can't make it!" Not only did I not want to shoot again, I moved away from the dreaded spot and over to my natural spot!

I have "spots" in my life other than sports. Maybe you call them "hot buttons." Some trigger positive responses and others trigger negative responses. Last year, I traveled thousands of miles to find a spot preinstalled and waiting for me. Wendy and I were in Hawaii celebrating our tenth wedding anniversary. I had seen to every detail of this trip and it was going to be perfect. Everything lined up: perfect weather, perfect convertible, perfect Maui — all for my perfectly beautiful wife!

We had just rented a Chrysler Sebring convertible. I handed the map to my copilot, Wendy, and we set off to find Maui's Hyatt Regency Resort. Then I came to a fork in the road. As soon as I turned right, it felt wrong, but I continued driving. Twenty miles later, a sign told us we had made a wrong turn.

That's when I ran over one of my spots — in Maui! I only had to hop on a plane, cross an ocean, rent a car and get lost to find it, but there it was in all of its negative glory! It was as if my mind had waited to run a program that was waiting for the right occasion: "Pete, when you get lost in a car, run!" I never saw it coming and it was too powerful to resist. It increased my blood pressure, sped up my pulse, started perspiration and increased irritation — all in one program! As a bonus, it caused my voice to take on a negative tone and my body language to sour. This masterpiece of design ran effectively and efficiently while attacking and repelling any human who came within range!

We all have spots that trigger responses and programs that have been written and stored for our use whenever we reach our spots. Certain people are your Keepers Of The Spot. All they have to do is open their mouths. Maybe your spots are situational, like the quiet lady who becomes a NASCAR driver when she gets cut off in traffic. Maybe your program runs when a store employee pushes your buttons with an attitude, look or comment. Or when someone questions your intelligence, experience or authority. Or when someone tells you that you aren't good enough.

Here are some suggestions that may help:
- Become aware of your spots.
- Have a new program ready to run when you hit a spot.
- Change your expectation to a desired, positive outcome when you hit your spot.
- Be prepared to work until you override your old programming.

You can do it. After all, if they're *your* buttons, guess who installed them?

If I had Hawaii to do all over again, this is the new program I would run:
- I make a wrong turn.
- I get lost.
- The spot where I discover I'm lost triggers this new, positive program: "You, my friend, have just gone 20 miles in the wrong direction. Isn't that great? You are with your

beautiful wife in one of the most romantic places in the world. You are in a sparkling new convertible, about to start a vacation on your tenth anniversary. You're traveling through beautiful scenery with nothing but time to enjoy the ride and the company. So stop, turn around, and enjoy spending 20 extra miles with your loving wife."

I will be prepared the next time I hit this spot, regardless of its location.

Family life is a particularly difficult place to be consistent. I'm not telling you to excuse your bad behavior. I just want to prepare you for the next time you see it. Don't feel like a failure and quit reaching, trying and stretching. Failure is an *event*, not a person — it is certainly not *you!*

I Want What I Want

My three-year-old son Jacob was happily playing with his new *Scooby-Doo Hot Wheels*, whizzing up and down the floors throughout the house. Six-year-old Gabriella heard the excitement and came running to see what was happening. Her opening salvo was, "Hey, why did *he* get those cool *Scooby-Doo Hot Wheels? I* didn't get any *Scooby-Doo Hot Wheels!* I want some."

I watched Jacob, who had been so carefree just minutes before, round up all five *Hot Wheels* and pull them tight to his body on the floor. He shrieked the dreaded word that all parents try to exorcise from their children's vocabulary: "MINE!"

I thought, "This is going to be a great teachable moment. I'm going to teach the joy of sharing to my children!" I began with the obvious: "Gabriella, you got the *Strawberry Shortcake* purse you wanted and Jacob got the *Hot Wheels* he wanted." She replied with the obvious: "I don't want this dumb old purse.

I want to play with the *Hot Wheels!*"

It would have been easy to say, "You mean the same purse you couldn't possibly live without just two hours ago? The same purse you asked me to put money in when you came home? The same purse you sang a song and danced a dance about? *That purse?*" I didn't — too obvious — but I thought it.

Instead, I moved to Obvious Solution Number Two: "Why don't you two just share?" My children may not know a lot, but they understand that "share" means "lose control of my stuff." Jacob clamped himself onto the *Hot Wheels,* causing me to make a decision worthy of Solomon: *Daddy is going to make you share!* I grabbed two *Hot Wheels* for Gabriella to play with, leaving Jacob three. (It was only fair to give him more; they were his *Hot Wheels!*)

Gabriella announced, "I don't want those! I hate those! I want the other ones!" (Mind you, we were not arguing over precious gems or rare stones.) I played the only card I had left, "Okay, *nobody* gets to play with *anything* until you two learn to share!" Both of them cried as the *Hot Wheels* were abandoned on the floor. Gabriella went to her room and Jacob went and cried to his Mother. "Perfect!" I thought to myself. All I wanted them to do was share!

Sometimes I can behave like Jacob, and wonderful Wendy can behave like Gabriella. When we want what we want, most of our arguments can be seen through the eyes of our children. I can get pretty one-sided about what I want. When I'm unable to understand where Wendy is coming from, she starts protecting her feelings and thoughts from me.

Many times in a disagreement, you may feel misunderstood and fear you'll be taken advantage of or have to give up your viewpoint or self-worth. Here's how it works:

- We want what we want.
- We want to be treated a certain way.
- We want to be communicated with in a certain way.
- We want to communicate with others in a certain way.
- We want life to move at a certain pace, sometimes slower and sometimes faster.
- We want some people to speed up.
- We want other people to slow down.
- We want our problems to be solved without conflict.
- We want others' problems to be solved, and if they experience a little conflict, so be it.
- We want some people to talk less.
- We want other people to talk more.
- We want information to be specific and to the point.
- We want information logical and factual and as plentiful as necessary to prove a point.
- We want some rules to be followed without question.
- We want other rules to be modified, changed or done away with all together.
- We want some things to change.
- We want other things to stay the same.

What do I want in customer service? Here are my rules:

- Regardless of whoever else may be shopping, I am the most important customer in the store.
- I want to be left alone when I'm looking and get immediate attention when I have a question.
- I want roomy aisles, squeaky clean buggies, wheels without defect, and checkout lines plentiful, short and fast.
- I want quality and quantity at low cost and a wide variety of goods and services, all on special.
- I want the store to be open around my schedule, and,

if I desired, to know they would close the store off for just me and my entourage.

As you can see, I don't want much! What if the stores you shop abandoned any attempt at customer service? What if you weren't important to them at all and every salesperson was rude and apathetic? What if quality was poor and quantity was minimal, aisles were cramped and crowded, service was slow, checkout lines narrowed down to one with a cashier slower than molasses, if they said your money wasn't welcome and they could replace you with a thousand other customers tomorrow? How much longer would you shop there?

Think how this applies in your home and work. Teachers, how's the customer service and rapport between you and your students? Bosses, what about your employees? Workers, what about your teams and leaders?

Remember what your parents said that didn't work on you? Chances are good that you're using the same tired lines on your juvenile "customers," too. It's all you've known! My special thanks go to Andy Andrews, business leader, speaker and bestselling author for granting permission to reprint his "50 Famous Parental Sayings" on the following page. They remind us how funny the "old tapes" sound when we blow off the dust, and how bittersweet it is to replay them today for others.

Because we have information our parents may have lacked, we have a new choice. Rather than controlling the people we love or those in our circle, we have the wonderful option of influencing them by matching what we *know* with what we *do!*

ANDY ANDREWS' FIFTY FAMOUS PARENTAL SAYINGS

You'd better CHANGE YOUR TUNE pretty quick or you're OUT OF HERE. I mean it. Is that understood? DON'T SHAKE YOUR HEAD at me. I can't hear your head rattle. Don't MUMBLE. You act as if the world OWES YOU a living. You've got a CHIP ON YOUR SHOULDER. You're NOT GOING ANYWHERE looking like that. YOU'RE CRAZY if you think you are. If you think you are, JUST TRY ME. I don't know WHAT'S WRONG WITH YOU. I never saw A KID LIKE YOU. Other kids don't pull stuff like that. I WASN'T LIKE THAT. What kind of an EXAMPLE do you think you are FOR YOUR BROTHERS AND SISTERS? Stand up straight. DON'T SLOUCH. Would you like a spanking? If you would LIKE A SPANKING, you tell me now and we'll get this thing over with. You're CRUISING FOR A BRUISING. I'm your father and as long as you live in my house, you'll DO AS I SAY. Do you think the RULES DON'T APPLY to you? I'm here to tell you they do. Are you blind? WATCH WHAT YOU'RE DOING. You walk around here like you're in a daze. Something better change and CHANGE FAST. You're driving your mother to an EARLY GRAVE. This is a family vacation. You're going to HAVE FUN whether you like it or not. Take some RESPONSIBILITY. Pull your own weight. Don't EXPECT OTHERS to pick up after you. And DON'T ASK ME for money. What, do you think I'm made of money? Do you think I have a tree that GROWS MONEY? You'd BETTER WAKE UP and I don't mean maybe. Do you act like this when you're away from us? We've GIVEN YOU EVERYTHING we possibly could. Food on the table. A roof over your head, things we never had WHEN WE WERE YOUR AGE. You treat us like we don't exist. That's NO EXCUSE. If he jumped off a cliff, would you JUMP OFF A CLIFF, too? You're GROUNDED. I'm not going to PUT UP WITH THIS for another minute. You're crazy if you think I am. If you think I am, JUST TRY ME. Don't look at me that way. LOOK AT ME when I'm talking to you. DON'T MAKE ME SAY THIS AGAIN!

Chapter 12:
STORIES OF INFLUENCE

"Do unto others as you would have them do unto you" is not a justification for treating people according to *our* comfort zones; it means just the opposite. You and I want to be treated as *individuals who matter,* and the Golden Rule says we should treat others as individuals, the "same" as we want them to treat us. Tony Alessandra, PhD, is author of *The Platinum Rule®*, which states, "Do unto others as *they* would have us do unto them." His idea is a wonderful attitude for increasing influence.

For instance, since we know that people do things for themselves, out of self-interest, let's help them do things that benefit them while benefiting others. Motivator Zig Ziglar teaches that we can have anything we want if we can help enough other people get what they want. I love this positive example:

The billionaire J. P. Morgan motivated his nephew, who was away at college, to answer letters from his frustrated mother (Morgan's sister). How? By pushing the student's "hot button." Morgan wrote a letter that ended with the words, "Enclosed please find $50," but enclosed nothing. Almost immediately, he received a reply from his nephew: "Uncle, the money you said was enclosed in your letter wasn't." Since the young man had "suddenly" discovered that the postal system operated in both directions, Morgan was able to get him to write home to his mother, too!

Another example, while effective, isn't nearly as positive: A little boy's mother heard him scream and left her housework to see if he had injured himself. She found him upstairs,

173

leaned over the crib of his baby sister, who was pulling his hair with a superbaby grip. The mother gently released the little girl's grip and explained to her son, "She's just a baby, Michael. She doesn't understand that pulling hair hurts." The mother was barely back at her chores when she heard the baby crying. "What's the matter with Jennifer?" she exclaimed as she rushed back into the nursery. Michael replied, "Nothing. Now she understands!"

As we draw to a close, I'd like to provide some positive, memorable examples to help you remember the power of *Influence*. They have made a difference in my life, and I hope they will in yours as well.

Faith, Belief And Desire

After an Open House for parents of students in our school, one of the fathers stayed behind to talk to me. Normally, when parents stay late, they are worried about their child and want to share their concerns. This time, however, the father wanted to tell me that I had made a difference in his daughter's life. Since her mother's death a few years before, she'd been unmotivated by school until she became a student in my class. He asked what I was doing in my classroom that had influenced his daughter so effectively.

Soon afterward, I injured my back and called on him — Dr. Charles Campbell, a highly respected chiropractor in our community. In conversation, I mentioned that I was writing a book about becoming an *Influencer, and he suggested that I meet Mike Penn, a commerical pilot and captain for Southwest Airlines. Through Dr. Campbell's influence, I connected with Mike, who agreed to meet me and share his story. And, because my father is my best friend, and I rarely do anything important without him, I invited him to come with me to meet Mike.

Like many other commercial pilots, Mike gained valuable experience and training in the military. Unlike most pilots, he was shot down, captured and forced to endure many hardships as a prisoner of war in Vietnam's infamous "Hanoi Hilton" prison. To get the obvious out of the way, he quickly asked and answered these three questions:

- *How long was I a prisoner?* 8 months.
- *What did I have to eat?* Soup, bread, some type of vegetable, and sugar and milk in the morning to maintain body weight.
- *Was I tortured?* He downplayed this, but yes. He added, "In the 70s, torture was not as harsh as earlier in the war."

Mike had successfully flown 124 combat missions, avoiding approximately 50 surface-to-air missiles. He explained that pilots literally engaged missiles in a dogfight — one-on-one, facing and defeating what could kill them. Pilots had to learn correct procedures and rely on what had been taught, removing fear as much as possible. I asked what a missile looks like coming at you. He replied, "The size of a telephone pole, as long and wide, but with fins to make it look scary. But, as in life, it's the ones you *don't* see that get you."

On August 6, 1972, Mike was stationed on the *USS Midway*, in the Gulf of Tonkin off the coast of North Vietnam. He'd just completed two night missions and was on his third combat mission of the day, making a major strike on Hai Phong. He and his wing man were isolated at the rear, in A7E Light Attack Jets, when a wave of surface-to-air missiles pierced the sky. He avoided the first set of two missiles, and a second pair, but a third set of two missiles did their job and struck the back of Mike's jet. His plane was going down in flames.

Over the Gulf, he realized the beach was eight miles away and his plane was picking up speed (400 knots, or 450 mph) as he headed toward the ground. "Even though you're taught to follow procedures in an emergency, survival instincts overcome training and logic. I should have gotten out much sooner, but all of my instincts kept me from ejecting."

Pilots find comfort and protection inside their plane, and the last place they want to be is outside their comfort zone. He held on so long that the jet's speed was dangerously high when he ejected, and the windblast was like running into a brick wall! He broke his leg and began a rapid descent to the ground. At that speed, his parachute should have malfunctioned or ripped apart, but it opened as he headed groundward.

From the air, Mike saw muzzle flashes. Groundfire was trying to kill him. He landed in a rice paddy next to a river, grabbed his radio, and called to his wing man, reporting that he was going to be there for a while. From behind, a villager hit him on the head and knocked him unconscious.

When he awoke, he saw that his elbows had been tied behind his back with his bootstraps. Nine villagers and one North Vietnamese soldier were standing in front of him. To them, he was a killer, a man who bombed their villages and should be killed. One tried to stab him. At the last moment, the North Vietnamese soldier intervened. But it was no act of mercy. As a pilot and soldier, Mike was worth more as a prisoner of war than dead. The enemy who would have killed Mike in open combat saved his life.

A boat ride, a truck ride and a water buffalo ride later, Mike was taken to the prison complex known to POWs as the Hanoi

Hilton. His captors had transported him on a water buffalo because his leg wouldn't support any weight. He received no medical treatment for his leg or neck injuries and arrived badly hurt. His throat was infected, and he spent the first three days in prison without a mosquito net. Consequently, by the second day, his eyes were swollen shut and his body was covered with mosquito bites. "I was so depressed that it saved my life," Mike told me. When prison guards asked him questions or tortured him, he was nonresponsive. "This state couldn't last, because you can live for a week without water, a month without food, but you can't live a second without a glimmer of hope." He saw two B-52 pilots die almost as soon as they gave up hope.

Just a few days into his captivity, he was locked in solitary confinement. Lying on the floor, he recalled his childhood and what had brought him to the U.S. Navy. As a little kid, he went to Dallas' Love Field to watch planes, dreaming of one day becoming a pilot. His father was an alcoholic and their relationship wasn't good.

When Mike was 15, the *Blue Angels* were flying their air show at the Naval Air Station in Dallas. He watched with excitement, and the pilots signed autographs after they landed. One of them asked Mike, "You want to fly one of these one day?" He replied, "Yes, sir!" The pilot grinned and said, "I suspect you will. See you next year!"

After another air show the following year, Mike found the same pilot. He began, "Sir, you probably don't remember...." Before he could finish, the man said, "Of course I remember you. You're going to fly one of these someday. Just remember to do it in the Navy."

From that day on, Mike's burning desire was to fly. Turning down a football scholarship, he received his degree in Political

Science from the University of Texas at Arlington while working full-time. He had only one dream in mind: flying jets. He told me, "I knew what I wanted!" and passed on this formula:

> ### It's all in your attitude:
> ### Your Thoughts + Your Emotions = Your Attitude

Mike added, "Throw in an overwhelming desire to succeed, and you have the formula to achieve all your dreams!"

The young graduate's next stop was Pensacola, Florida, for Officer Training School. (If you've seen the Richard Gere film, *An Officer and a Gentleman,* you are familiar with the program.) I asked him what the officer training program was like, and he explained, 'It was fast-paced to the point that they gave you too many things to do and not enough time to do them." Marine Corps Drill Instructors were very intimidating — their yelling alone produced too much mental stress for some. How had he made it through? "I was fortunate that my roommate had already completed a training program at Virginia Military Institute but opted not to go into the Air Force or Army. He wanted to be in the Navy and fly." This person changed Mike's attitude. Whenever stress became too much, his roommate would say, "Water off a duck's back! Don't worry about it, and move on." His insights made the difference for Mike, who ranked first in his class and graduated to become an officer.

His first assignment was Attack Squadron 56, on the *USS Midway.* His first commanding officer (CO), Mike said, was the purest leader he had ever encountered — a man who:

- Led by example — a leader who wouldn't ask you to do anything he was not willing to do himself.
- Any man could wish was his father.
- Mike named his second son after.

After Mike's first combat briefing, the CO said to this new pilot, "Here's what we'll do, Mike. You're going to see three things: Migs (enemy planes), anti-aircraft fire and surface-to-air missiles. I want you to be my wing man. Don't leave my wing the entire mission. I'll get you back. I'll dodge all the missiles, all the fire and anything else that comes along. You just stay on my wing and trust me, and I'll get you back alive."

Mike struggled to explain the intensity of this relationship: "You develop such a trust in your fellow pilots, there's nothing I can compare it to."

Returning from that first mission, the CO asked Mike if he had seen the missiles taking off against them. He replied, "I didn't see *anything* but the wing of your plane!" Because I wanted to learn more about the CO and his leadership style, I asked Mike for other examples. The CO was a leader everyone respected, the only skipper known to actually sit and talk with junior officers. On one occasion, a junior officer was called to fly immediately after flying several missions in a row. When he said, "I have to fly again, but I'm mentally wasted," the CO got on the phone and ordered, "Take him off this mission. I'll fly it myself." Those who served under him would do anything *not* to make him look bad. The commanding officer was a leader who understood influence.

This history was vivid in Mike's mind as he remained in solitary confinement. He didn't want his six-month-old son to grow up without a father. He focused on it constantly, and it became his passion to survive. He decided to take charge of his destiny and live! He repeated to himself, "I want to live, I want to survive." He thought back to obstacles he had overcome until that point and drew on that strength. It became his glimmer of hope and his link to life. He pictured his wife and son.

Prisoners called the solitary section "Heartbreak Hotel." Picture a large box with a hallway down the middle and eight 7x7-foot squares, four on each side of the hallway. Mike was in the last cell on the end. Prisoners communicated by tapping out codes learned in survival training.

After weeks, Mike was put in a room with the other Americans. He said, "From that day on, my faith grew and grew. I was so happy just to see another person." As a pilot, he was taught to think he was invincible, but he learned you can't survive alone — you can always do more and better as a team. I never fully appreciated what teamwork was until I heard Mike talk about his isolation. You never again take team members for granted once you are truly alone and can't pull them alongside.

American prisoners developed a bond so unbreakable that they shared everything with one another: their hopes, desires, beliefs, struggles, concerns and weaknesses. Nothing was too personal in their sacred bond. They shared three important, personal definitions of what matters in life:
- *Faith*: believing without seeing.
- *Belief*: accepting the information given in combat school, using it, and knowing they weren't going to die.
- *Desire*: an overwhelming sense that they would succeed.

In solitary, Mike felt as low and discouraged as possible. Military training made him feel invincible, but faith in God brought him humility. He says that, without humility, it's almost impossible to have faith in God; that humility can be found after you are broken, and that when you become broken and humble, there is only one way to go — *up!*

He speaks often to parents on this topic of "Faith, Belief and Desire." So I was so excited to hear his comments about influencing young people, even in the middle of his war story:

- Children will ask us 80,000 questions about life. It is imperative that we listen to them and answer them. If we listen to them when they're young, they'll listen to us when they're older. If we talk with them when they're young, they'll talk to us when they're older. If we support them when they're young, they'll support us when they're older. If we show them love when they're young, they'll show us love when they're older.
- Kids need us more when they're teenagers than at any other time. In trying to become adults, they model what they've seen and, as adults, we become frustrated with them. Teens don't do what we say; they do what we do. They are confused by behavior they have witnessed.
- Teach kids that there is no use in arguing. As adults, the difference in *arguing* and *discussing* is our attitude. If our attitude is negative, it becomes an argument. If our attitude is positive, it remains a discussion. Arguing is a lot like trying to start your car with your horn — you can make a lot of noise, but you won't get anywhere!

Mike explained that love for our children is unconditional in healthy families. If our kids misbehave, we still love them. If they let us down, we still love them. Our ability *not* to put conditions on our love is one of the most important things we can ever do as influencing parents.

Eight months later, Mike was released. His first stop was Oakland Hospital, but before he was admitted, his commanding officer was the first to meet him. Holding Mike's flight gear in his hands, he said, "I have a plane waiting for you, and you're going to fly it, so put this stuff on." Because of his CO's faith in him, Mike was the first POW to fly again. On his first flight, Mike had been his CO's wing man. On this flight, his CO served as Mike's wing man. Again a true leader, the CO was able to lead or follow. He could be both the teacher *and* the student. The two flew together and practiced dog-fighting in the skies before returning home. "He had complete faith in me. He trusted me enough to fly with me after everything I had experienced. I'm thankful I was to be taught humility, positive attitude, faith, belief and desire by that man."

As his story wound down, Mike reminisced, "I think back to when I met the *Blue Angels* pilot. I was just a kid standing at the front of the crowd when he called me over to ask if I wanted to fly one day. I remember him saying, 'I suspect you will.' His positive attitude, faith, belief and desire began a dream in me that one day came true."

Mike smiled, knowing he had saved the best part of his story for last: "By the way, the *Blue Angels* pilot at that air show became my commanding officer in the war! I can still hear him telling me, 'Of course I remember you, and you're going to fly one of these someday. Just remember to do it in the Navy!'"

Influence: A Grandfather's Legacy

Bingiee Shiu, a music teacher at Memorial High School in Houston, received *The Sunshine Award* for the inspired difference he makes in the lives of students and faculty. He has received many awards in his career. After I describe him as a phenomenal teacher and gifted musician, I run out of superlatives. In accepting the prize, he shared this story about influence:

The Bible tells us the sins of fathers follow their sons from generation to generation. I wonder if it holds true for the good things fathers do as well? This is story about a Chinese grandfather, his son and the son's son.

The Grandfather was very powerful in the feudal system that dominated prerevolutionary China. Powerful, yet good to "his people" at a time when "class" meant status and "rank" was a symbol of life, the Grandfather displayed these and more. He had a compassionate heart, because he had learned that life's material prizes are not the most important; human life is much more valuable.

China's wealthy landlords owned castles, farmland as far as the eye could see and even the people who worked the land. Landlords built their monumental homes in the safety of the mountains, at the top of the world. When attacked, they closed the gates of their domain and remained safely protected within their walls.

Powerful and wealthy, the Grandfather allowed the peasants, his laborers who lived at the base of the mountain, to seek refuge within his castle's protective walls. Whenever scouts warned of an enemy's approach, the peasants knew they could run up the mountain to safety. The Grandfather won the hearts of his people, and in later years, would have an impression even on those beyond his domain.

His son's early years were privileged. He attended private school on the island of Macau, another world in those days, because the Grandfather wanted the best for his son. The son traveled by boat to the island for school, and during holidays, he journeyed back home across the seas. On one voyage, his Grandfather's influence saved his life.

At that time, piracy was rampant on the high seas. Pirates stopped the ship on which the boy was sailing, demanding more than anyone really wanted to give up. When they discovered the boy's identity, born to this great man who had done so much good for others, they released both the ship and its passengers unharmed. Honoring the Grandfather, they sent all on their way without loss. It was *not the sins of the father that those men remembered, but his great deeds and how he treated others.*

Later in life, the son's fortune changed. War eventually caught up to the family, separating the Grandfather and his son, and they never saw each other again. Eventually, the son settled in America, where life offered many possibilities but required work and determination. Young Chinese men were not easily accommodated into American society. Back then, minorities possessed no power. There was no talk of men joining hands across lines of racial prejudice. Life was difficult for those with darker skin.

But the young man had learned from his father's example. When he first arrived in America, he spoke no English. Completing four years in college, he had become very popular among his classmates and graduated at the top of his class. He bridged at least some of the gap.

The son went on to become a very successful physician, treating patients from all parts of the world who heard about his skill and intelligence. Most of all, they heard he was a man of compassion. If he was unable to heal a patient, the son (we'll call him the Doctor in our story) worked even harder and refused to give up. He always found time for his patients, in his schedule and in his heart.

During his years in medical practice, the Doctor worked diligently and received both financial and professional rewards. From the Grandfather — his father — he had learned that wealth means little if it is not shared. So he gave generously to his college and church. He established a nursing scholarship at the hospital, making it possible for gifted students to learn the healing arts without the added burden of paying for their education. One cold winter evening, he and his wife purchased blankets from stores until the back of their car was overflowing, and then drove to a street corner in the poorest section of town to give them away to people in need. No catches or conditions, just un-selfish sharing.

When the Doctor announced his retirement, patients scrambled to get just one last office visit with him. They knew his time was limited, and many wept as they left for the last time. He had always told his own son that his dream was to make enough money in his practice to sup-port himself as a medical missionary, giving comfort to people who otherwise couldn't afford a doctor — patients outside his social and economic circle. In retirement, he would be able to do good, share with his family and make small, effective contributions to his world.

People needn't win a Nobel Prize to do good in the world. We don't have to make the evening news to affect some-one else's life. The lives of the Grandfather and the Doctor — my Grandfather and his son, who became my father — have proven this. It's not just a story; it's my true legacy.

So why does this teacher — the Grandson — read Chicken Soup for the Soul *to his music classes? Why does he en-courage you to recognize random acts of kindness in our world? It's because he thinks you have a lot to offer this world and he believes in your generation. He has to, be-cause your generation is going to mold the world in which my sons will live. In this way, I make another small contri-bution to my sons, and I hope to continue my grandfather's legacy.*

Mr. Shiu was honored because he understands and passes his legacy along every day. He never knew his grandfather ex-cept through his father's stories. And you now know them all. The legacy of all three men is their lasting influence.

The Garden, My Dad And Me

You know that, as a teen, I struggled with understanding my father. Learning about personality styles helped me connect with him when I learned how **C**s think. Now I give him plenty of time when I ask him a question. It isn't easy because I want the information as soon as possible, but I also want to get the best results!

My dad sees life from a different perspective, and it would be arrogant to believe that my viewpoint is the only one that counts. So I plan ahead before I make a big decision. I call my dad a week early and share what I'm thinking about, so he has time to think about the dynamics and analyze the possible solutions. When I call, he gives me his analysis. It's really handy to have someone in my life who thinks like he does!

I am privileged to have a dad I can communicate with in this way, which I appreciated even more when he underwent heart surgery a few years ago. I promised myself that, when he healed, I'd do something I had been thinking about for 10 years.

Dad is a Master Gardner by certification and by experience. He works in his garden year-round, but I never took advantage of his homegrown wisdom. So, when planting season came around, I decided that was the year I'd work with him in the garden. His response to my announcement was, "See you this weekend!" As soon as we began, I started appreciating everything I had learned about our personality style differences.

My assignment was clearing the 10 walking areas between the rows, each about 20 feet long. Dad's a natural gardener, using very few chemicals. These walking areas consist of compost, newspaper, leaves — anything that can degrade over the growing and harvesting period, so he can recycle the soil and nutrients for the planting season.

Up for the challenge, I began at my usual pace: lightspeed. The shovel had hit the ground five times before Dad said, "Son, you'd better pace yourself or you're going to burn out." I thought, "Don't tell me what to do, oldtimer!" but I said, "I'll be okay." He shrugged and kept working. We had only been working together five minutes and I was already irritated!

I took a deep breath and resumed, but I kept hearing in my head, "Take your time; you're going to burn out!" I went at it harder and faster and soon realized I'm not 18 anymore. Pacing might prevent passing out! I finished my walking areas in about an hour, while Dad was just completing his first row. I collapsed in a chair, harassing him for going so slow. He laughed and took most of the morning to finish, and I pitched in when needed.

Then came the awesome insight that helped convince me of the value to be found in understanding personality styles: I had made it through the morning without wanting to kill him and was looking forward to planting seeds and small vegetables! We knelt side by side and started to plant. I watched closely and planted carefully just the way he did: same depth and amount of soil, creating a lip of dirt around each plant.

Dad was pleased. Normally, I would have done it my way, but he had a reason for planting exactly as he did. Who was I to question more than 50 years of gardening wisdom?

We finished planting and started watering. I asked, "So, how long before we see some results?"

"Ohhhhh, about three months."

"Three months? Are you kidding?" At that moment, I knew that, if I were a farmer, my family would starve. Who in the world waits three months to eat a tomato? I asked, "Can you speed up the process?"

He said, "You can go to the store...." (That was a pretty good one for a **C**!) He explained that nature doesn't work that way. You have to be patient and steady.

I learned more that day than what it takes to plant a garden. I confirmed that my *fast-paced* desire for immediate results works only in certain situations. I can't control nature! My gardener dad understands that he can influence the result by doing it the better way. He stays with a project and sees it through. His garden will always provide him more rewards than I will receive until I consistently think and behave as he does in that environment. And I thought I was just going to spend a day in the garden with my dad!

Wendy Still Teaches Me

I've shared many stories about interactions between my wife and me. I believe strongly that our ability to communicate according to our personality styles has helped our marriage succeed. We often speak in **DISC** language to each other.

At the end of a school year, teachers experience pressure. Wendy was in the middle of a pressure-packed week, and on Friday, she just wanted to come home and relax. When I walked in the door, I knew I was going to hear a long story about pain and stress. In **D** mode, I began doing what I thought would help, telling her how to solve her problem. I spoke quickly, directly and to the point. She stopped me mid-sentence. "Honey, could you just not be a **D** at all this weekend?"

This was her way of saying, "I need you to slow down, be softer, and just listen." Before we learned the **DISC** language, Wendy had no way to say this without offending me. Now we both know what our strengths and struggles are, and she needed less **D** and more **S** from me. I did my best to adjust my style. I recommend learning this early in your marriage so you can benefit as Wendy and I do every day. John McNaughton wrote:

> **Maturity begins to grow when you can sense your concern for others outweighing your concern for yourself.**

That night, Wendy and I watched TV before going to sleep. The show focused on teenage girls and their eating disorders. We watched the daily routines of a young woman, filling herself with food and throwing up what she had eaten.

I wasn't paying attention to Wendy's response because I was caught up in my own intense reaction. I "saw" some of the teenagers I worked with every day and wanted to learn more so I could attack their problem and help them. The more I saw, the more I felt that no teenager should have to deal with this! I wanted to save them all. I would take on the scourge of bulimia and save one teenage girl at a time!

Then I noticed that Wendy was lying on her side, crying softly. My first "guy response" was that I should run my old *Stop Crying* program on Weepy Wendy. I hesitated as I thought, "Pete, you talk to people all the time about influence and how to communicate effectively with others. How is doing what you've always done going to serve Wendy? How about doing what you should for the person who deserves it most?" This was an easy discussion in my mind. I had no objection, but how should I respond?

Okay, let's work through it. Why was Wendy crying? I realized that she has a strong **S** and **I** bent and was probably thinking about our own little Gabrielle, imagining the pain our daughter might experience at 15. This emotion is less likely in a **D** dad like me, but **S** types live in a state of worry, especially about things that seem out of their control regarding people they love. Wendy didn't need my **D**-style "love and compassion." I did something I never thought I could: I became soft and sensitive. (Some people call this an "Alan Alda moment.") I closed my mouth, reached out, and patted her until she stopped crying.

If we had been two **D**s that night, we would have started a crusade to rid the world of this pain. But Wendy isn't a **D** at all, and she needed my love and understanding. All my "we've gotta do something" energy would not have soothed her pain. So I equalized my style by lowering my **D** and raising my **S**.

Pat, pat, pat away. Of course it felt like an eternity to me at the time, but it was one of the best uses of my time since we've been married. How interesting that I could get worked up about rescuing someone I didn't know on television when I almost missed someone struggling within my reach.

I hope these stories of ordinary people have helped you see that we all need to be understood, and how ordinary people can do extraordinarily simple things to make that happen. We can either influence people positively or we can control them negatively. Control may work in the short term, but it destroys relationships in the end.

Your real choice is to what level you would like to build your *Influencer Incorporated* company. It's your company and your life. You have the ability to go global with both. Start today, right where you are.

Welcome to the school of life, where there's a new test every day!

190

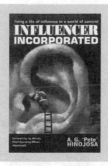

MEET PETE

Author A. G. "Pete" Hinojosa combines his practical classroom teaching knowledge with personal experience to connect with audiences of all ages and backgrounds.

He has been:

- Selected three times as an Outstanding Secondary Educator in the Nation
- Recognized five times by *Who's Who in American High School Teachers*
- Rated in the top 2% of high school teachers in the country
- Honored by students at Kingwood High School in Houston, Texas, when they have voted him the Funniest, Most Enthusiastic, and Best Teacher.

Customized seminar presentations and development of unique human behavior materials for companies and school districts are Pete's specialty. He is an Advanced Certified Behavior Consultant and coauthor of several books, including *A+ Ideas for Students' Success* (with Robert A. Rohm, PhD) and *Y-Zup*, a book for teens. *Influencer Incorporated* is his most recent book.

Pete is currently the Community Network Coordinator for Spring Branch Independent School District, where he works with businesses, administrators, teachers, parents and students across 42 schools. He still teaches every day for Spring Branch Independent School District's 40-plus schools.

For speaking and consulting projects, reach Pete through his web site: *www.apurposefuljourney.com.*